PROBATE

THE RIGHT WAY TO PROVE A WILL

By the same author:
Write Your Own Will

Available as a paperfront

PROBATE

THE RIGHT WAY TO PROVE A WILL

KEITH BEST T.D., M.A. (Oxon.)
of the Inner Temple, Barrister-at-Law.

RIGHT WAY

TO MY WIFE
ELIZABETH

CONTENTS

Life Insurance Policies — Business Property
Relief — Agricultural Property Relief —
Woodlands Relief — Death on Active Service
— Death at the Same Time — One Death
after Another — Subsequent Fall in Value —
How Much Inheritance Tax Payable —
Payment of Inheritance Tax — Preparation of
an Account — How to Raise the Money —
Authority to Release Funds — National
Savings — The Interview — Releasing the
Assets — Payment by Instalments — Giving
Property Instead — Saving on Professional
Charges.

Introduction

Death is something that none of us likes to talk about and yet it is the one thing that we can be sure will happen. Moreover, almost certainly, anyone who has a family will have to face up to the death of a relative.

The occasion of a death of a loved one or friend can be extremely distressing, yet there are many things that have to be done when a person dies. Some of these have to be done quite quickly and the object of this book is to try to help those people who suddenly find themselves confronted with a death and who may be at a loss to know what to do.

Although you may not have need of this book straightaway I hope that you will read it so that you will have a general knowledge of what has to be done when the unfortunate occasion arises. In doing this you will be preparing yourself so that you can deal competently with the death of someone when you will be suffering a great emotional disturbance. If you follow the advice in this book then the death of someone in the future, from an administrative point of view, should hold no fear for you.

The book tells you how you can apply for Probate (where there is a Will) or Letters of Administration (where there is no Will) without employing a solicitor. There are many circumstances, however, where the services of a solicitor will be not only helpful but necessary. A solicitor's fees for administering an estate come out of the estate itself, that is, the money and assets that have been left by the dead person.

Consequently, as the personal representative of the dead person or as the one whom the dead person appointed in his/her Will as Executor, in administering the estate, you will not have to pay the solicitor's fees yourself — they are an expense which can come out of the assets of the estate. Once you have an idea of the value of the total money and assets that were left by the dead person then any solicitor will give you an estimate of what his fees would be if he were asked to deal with the estate.

In the case of a simple estate you will not have to employ a solicitor at all since you will be able to do everything by following the advice in this book, but there are certain circumstances where it would be advisable to consult a solicitor.

It may be that the deceased person when writing his/her Will thought that his/her estate was worth more than it really was. This could mean that there is insufficient money in the estate to satisfy specific gifts or legacies to various people which have been set out in the Will. More usually the value of the estate will be far greater than the specific gifts or legacies contained in the Will in which case the amount left over is known as the residue and, usually, there is a provision in the Will stating how the residue is to be dealt with.

Another situation in which you should consult a solicitor is if the deceased left debts which were greater than the value of his estate, in other words, the estate is insolvent.

Hopefully, when you read the Will, there will not only be sufficient assets in the estate to satisfy payment of all the gifts or legacies in the Will but also all the provisions of the Will can be understood fully and are perfectly clear in their meaning. You are very much in the hands of the deceased person here because all will depend upon whether he/she used simple language conveying a definite meaning which is not capable of misinterpretation. It may be that he/she will have read the book "Write Your Own Will" (by the same author) in which case, if all the advice contained in that book has been followed, there should be no difficulty!

The sort of problem that can arise, however, is where, for example, there is a provision in the Will for a gift of a sum of money to be given to a named person, say Tom Jones. No difficulty occurs if there is only one Tom Jones who was known to the deceased person but, in the absence of any further description of Tom Jones, such as giving his address or his relationship to the deceased, there is a major problem if the deceased person knew two or more people who were called Tom Jones. As the Executor of the deceased person's Will you are responsible for administering the estate and making payments to persons entitled to them under the provisions of the Will and in such a case it would be advisable to consult a solicitor as he will be able to help you decide to which Tom Jones the payment should be made. Even then, of course, the matter might be challenged in a Court of Law.

You may wish to employ a solicitor or your Bank to deal with the estate because you are too busy or do not have sufficient confidence to do it yourself. In the case of a simple estate you should not have to spend too much time on it and it is hoped that by reading this book you will feel able to do the matter yourself even though you lacked confidence before-hand. If you do consult a solicitor for these reasons, however, you should remember that the cost of the solicitor has to come out of the estate as is mentioned above and, usually, it comes out of the residue of the estate which is what is left of the estate once all the specific gifts or legacies have been paid.

It may be that you are the person entitled to receive the residue of the estate under the terms of the Will but if the person entitled to receive the residue is someone else, then it is his share of the estate which will be diminished by the solicitor's fees being paid out of it.

Naturally, if the deceased person had complicated business affairs, had his own firm, or was in business together with other people then you would do well to seek the help of a solicitor. Likewise, where there is settled property that is part of the estate of the deceased person, such as the case where

Trusts have been set up.

Where a deceased person has not left a Will then the Law of Intestacy determines the way in which the assets of the estate should be distributed. This is explained in later chapters of this book and there should be no difficulty where the relative or relatives who are entitled to receive the estate are known both as to their identity and where they are living. If neither their identity nor their location are known, however, then once again, you should consult a solicitor.

I hope that all this has not put you off trying to go it alone and I suggest that you now read on and discover that it is not nearly as complicated as you might have thought.

1

The Circumstances of Death

There are so many different ways and places in which death can occur; in the home either suddenly or after a prolonged illness, in hospital, in a road traffic accident or in an accident at work. You should turn to Chapter 10, page 75 in order to discover what happens when somebody in Scotland dies.

Controversy has raged for a long time and will no doubt continue to do so over the precise point at which it can be said that clinical death occurs. Very often we see reports in newspapers of people who have been so severely injured that their brain can be said to be dead but their bodies are still alive even if this is due entirely to life-support machines. Such discussions are outside the scope of this small book and I have assumed that you, the reader, will accept the judgment of a doctor as to whether a person has died or not.

Naturally, matters such as the removal of organs for therapeutics, or medical research, are much more easily administered if the death occurs in hospital rather than at home but, fundamentally, the situation is no different in that both at hospital and at home a doctor will need to be present in order to pronounce the person dead.

Matters of Immediate Concern

It may well be that the person who has died has expressed a wish that one or more of the organs of the body should be used for spare-part surgery or other therapeutic uses.

Obviously, it is important that quick action is taken here since, in order to be used, the organs will have to be removed within a few hours of death. This is particularly true of the eyes. The person who is entitled to possession of the body, usually the next of kin, can authorise the removal of eyes unless he believes that the dead person had an objection, or the surviving spouse or other relative objects. The removal is done by a doctor who must have satisfied himself that the person is dead. Where a person dies in hospital then an officer of the hospital can authorise removal if a dead person expressed his desire that this was his wish either in writing, or by declaration in the presence of two witnesses during the illness from which he died.

The person who has died may have made his intention quite clear that he wished his organs to be used after his death by stating this in writing. Alternatively, he may carry a kidney donor card. These kidney donor cards can be obtained from most doctors' surgeries and increasing numbers of people are carrying them on their person so that, in the event of a violent death, such as in a road traffic accident, it will be quite obvious to the hospital authorities that the person wished his kidneys to be used.

Sometimes a person may have written in his Will that he wished his organs to be used after his death. This is fine, so long as the next of kin knows about it. Otherwise, by the time the Will is found and read it will be too late for any organs to be removed from the body and used.

As far as leaving the body for the purposes of medical education or research is concerned the local hospital will be able to advise suitable arrangements for this. The surviving husband or wife or nearest relative can object to a person's body being used in this way and can ask for a burial or cremation without this happening. You should talk to the hospital doctor.

Before the body can be removed for these purposes a death certificate and notice to the Inspector of Anatomy must be completed. The procedure is for the next of kin to contact immediately the Inspector of Anatomy in London, or the Professor of Anatomy at the nearest Medical School, who will arrange to have the body collected and will provide the forms if they have not been obtained already. There need be no fear of organs being removed when a person is still alive if a body is left for medical science or therapeutics since, under the Human Tissue Act, 1961, no removal of any organ can take place until a registered medical practitioner has satisfied himself that death has occurred.

Decisions such as these, obviously, have to be taken fairly quickly. Nevertheless, if possible, it is always better to have a copy of the dead person's Will since, very often, there may be certain instructions contained in the Will about the removal of organs and disposal of the body and, in some cases, the desire of the dead person to have his body examined by other persons after his death to ensure that he will not be buried alive. The safeguards against this happening, however, are such as to render such a concern somewhat groundless.

What Happens to the Body?

The person entitled to possession of the deceased's body is, where there is a Will, the Executor and, where there is no Will, the next of kin. Although most Executors would want to dispose of the deceased's body in accordance with the wishes of the deceased expressed in the Will, nevertheless, any such directions expressed in the Will are not mandatory and it is entirely a matter for the Executor as to how the body is disposed of. By the Anatomy Act 1832 it is lawful for any Executor or other party having lawful possession of the body of any deceased person to permit the body of such deceased person to undergo anatomical examination. However, if either in writing or at any time during his life or orally in the presence of two or more witnesses during his last illness, the deceased person has stated that his body should *not* be used for such an examination after his death, then it must not. In addition, the surviving husband or wife or any known relative can object to the use of the body in this way, in which case it cannot undergo anatomical examination.

Likewise, if the deceased has expressed his desire, either in writing or orally in the presence of two or more witnesses during his last illness, that his body *should* be used for anatomical examination then, so long as this desire is made known to the person who has lawful possession of the dead body, that person must direct that such examination should take place subject, again, to any objection by the deceased person's surviving husband or wife or nearest known relative.

By the Human Tissue Act 1961 it is provided that "if any person, either in writing at any time or orally in the presence of two or more witnesses during his last illness has expressed a request that his body or any specified part of his body be used for therapeutic purposes or for purposes of medical education or research, the person lawfully in possession of his body after his death may, unless he has reason to believe that the request was subsequently withdrawn, authorize the removal from the body of any part or, as the case may be, the specified part, for use in accordance with the request".

The general rule, therefore, that an Executor can dispose of the body as he wishes, is subject to the Anatomy Act and the Human Tissue Act. For a long time this situation has been regarded as unsatisfactory and there have been some attempts to have the law changed.

Obtaining the Death Certificate

A death must be notified to the local Registrar of Births and Deaths. The Register has to be signed in his presence by either a relative of the deceased present at the death or in attendance during the last illness, or some other relative. If there are no relatives then the Register can be signed by a person present at the death or the occupier of the house in which it occurred or, failing that, by somebody living in the house.

If a person other than a relative is the one who is registering the death then it must be the person who is going to be responsible for disposal of the body. Within five days of the death either the actual registration has to be made or written notice of a death has to be sent to the Registrar. The dead person's doctor should send a Certificate of the cause of death to the Registrar as well as giving written notice of this to the person who will be registering the death.

There is a small charge for obtaining a Death Certificate and the body cannot be disposed of until either the Registrar has certified that he has registered or had notice of the death, or the Coroner has made a disposal order. The latter situation will arise where there is an inquest into the death. The Coroner has to be informed if there is anything unusual about a death and in all cases where death is caused by an accident or where the cause is unknown or where there is anything suspicious about it. In addition, he has to be informed if death occurs during an operation in hospital, or in prison, or where there is likely to have been suicide, and where alcohol, drugs, poisoning or abortion may have been the cause. An inquest has to be held where violence or unnatural causes have resulted in death. The Registrar cannot register a death until he has been authorized by the Coroner once the Coroner becomes involved.

Where the Coroner is satisfied that there is nothing untoward about the death then he gives formal notice to the Registrar so that the death can be registered and a disposal certificate can be issued in order that the funeral may proceed. Where the Coroner is not satisfied, however, he can order a post mortem or an inquest or both. In Scotland an inquest is known as a public inquiry and, although there are no Coroners, violent deaths in Scotland are investigated by the

Procurator Fiscal.

If the death is not registered within five days or within fourteen days where written notice of the death has been sent to the Registrar, he may require a relative, person present at the death, occupier or other resident of the house in which the death occurred to attend at the Registry to give the necessary details. It is an offence not to comply with such a requirement. If a death has not been registered within twelve months of its occurrence then the Registrar General has to give his consent for it to be registered.

Stillbirth

A child who dies after birth is registered as a death but a stillbirth is where a child is born dead after at least 28 weeks of pregnancy. A stillbirth must be registered as a birth and a certificate, signed by the doctor or midwife who was present at the birth or who has examined the body of the child, must be produced to the Registrar. The certificate must state the cause of death and the estimated duration of the pregnancy where this is possible. A stillbirth may only be registered within three months of the birth.

If no doctor or midwife is present then anyone present can make a declaration on Form 35 which is obtainable from the Registrar stating that to the best of his or her knowledge the child was stillborn. If there is any doubt that the child was born dead then the coroner must be informed so that he can make his investigations.

The death of a foetus before the 28th week of pregnancy is a miscarriage which is not registered.

Death at Sea

A death at sea is recorded in the Ship's log and the entry witnessed by a crew member and, if possible, a doctor. This is a valid registration of death although forms have to be completed later in order that relatives can obtain a copy of the registration of death. The Captain of the ship has the right to bury a body on his own authority although, naturally, he will try to contact the relatives if they are not on board and discover their wishes.

Death Abroad

When a person dies abroad the death is registered according to the law of the country in which the death takes place. It is a good idea to register the death with the British Consul in the country in order that copies of the death certificate can be obtained from the Registrar at St. Catherine's House, 10, Kingsway, London, WC2B 6JP. A death certificate will be needed to bring the body back to this country.

Death of a Serviceman Abroad

When a serviceman dies abroad the Ministry of Defence will arrange and pay for the funeral in that country. If the family wish the body to be flown home then the Ministry of Defence will do this but the family is then responsible for the funeral arrangements, although the Ministry of Defence will provide the coffin and make a small contribution towards the expenses.

There are special regulations for registering the death of a member of the armed forces and a death occurring on one of Her Majesty's ships or aircraft. Where a seaman dies whilst serving or within six months of serving in certain circumstances, the Department of Trade is empowered to deal with any of his property either on the ship or in any country outside the U.K. The Department of Trade can distribute such property between the next-of-kin, the seaman's widow or child (including both adopted and illegitimate), any persons entitled to the property under the seaman's Will and any creditors.

Funeral Arrangements

Naturally, one of the first things that has to be done is the arrangement of the funeral and disposal of the body either by cremation or burial. The deceased may have had a specific desire as to the nature of the funeral and disposal of the body and this is likely to be included in his/her Will. Consequently, before arranging the funeral you should look at the Will. In most cases the relatives of the deceased would want to abide by such a desire although there is nothing in law to oblige them to do so.

Although it is not necessary, it is usual to seek the assistance of a Funeral Director and a list can be found under the heading "Funeral Directors" in Yellow Pages of the Telephone Directory or from advertisements in local papers.

You can visit a Funeral Director to discuss what arrangements you wish to make and to discover what services are available. These should include a hearse and a car for mourners, moving the body from the house, embalming, keeping the body in the chapel of rest and burial or cremation. Any general information about funerals or funeral directors may be obtained from the National Association of Funeral Directors, 618, Warwick Rd., Solihull, W. Midlands (tel 021-711-1343), whose members subscribe to a code of practice which includes offering a simple basic funeral, giving a written estimate, having price lists freely available and accepting their Association's complaints procedure.

If a person has no money then the Local Authority or hospital will undertake the funeral and this will happen if a person dies in hospital and there are no relatives to pay for the funeral.

If the person making the funeral arrangements and/or his/her partner is receiving Income Support, Family Credit or Housing Benefit and has savings of less than £500 (£1,000 if the claimant is aged 60 or over) then a payment for funeral expenses can be claimed. This is made as a right and is not discretionary. Get an estimate or bill from a funeral director. You can apply for the payment at any time up to three months after the funeral, even after you have paid the bill, but it is always better if you can claim before paying it. The payment is for the basic costs of a simple funeral. Money which has been left by the deceased may have to be taken into account and the DSS will normally recover the payment from the estate if there is money available. You make a claim on form SF200 available at DSS offices. The following costs can be claimed: documents such as death certificates, a plain coffin, transport for the coffin and bearers plus one additional car, reasonable cost of flowers, undertaker's fees and gratuities, chaplain's, organist's, cemetery or crematorium fees for a simple funeral or cremation, the cost of any additional expenses as a result of the religious faith of the deceased up to £75, the reasonable travelling costs of one return journey within the UK either to arrange or attend the funeral, the costs of transporting the deceased to either his/her home or the undertakers from anywhere within the UK.

A funeral payment is not made if the funeral takes place abroad nor will the DSS pay for the cost of bringing the body back to the UK.

Every Christian has a theoretical right to be buried in the churchyard of his/her home parish, subject to there being room, irrespective of where the death took place. The priest or vicar will be able to tell you if there is room, the fee for burial and if permission will be given for a headstone. The Church of England has set fees for a funeral service and burial. The local Town Hall will know if there is a Local Authority cemetery nearby and the fee for a grave there. You should check the Will to see if the deceased has arranged a space in a churchyard or cemetery. Burial elsewhere needs special permission.

For a cremation five forms have to be filled in. This is to

ensure that cremation, which is a final act, does not take place until everything that needs to be done with the body, such as establishing the cause of death, has been completed. Form A (application form) is signed by the next-of-kin or Executor. Forms B and C (cremation certificates) are each signed by a different doctor, the second confirming that of the doctor who last attended the deceased. There is a charge for these. If the death is referred to the Coroner these two forms are replaced by Form E (certificate for cremation) which can be sent directly to the funeral director by the coroner. Form F is signed by the doctor for the crematorium. Finally, the Certificate for Burial or Cremation, which is issued by the Registrar, is not required if the Coroner has issued Form E.

The Department of Social Security produce a most helpful booklet D49 "What to do after a death" which can be obtained from the bereavement officer in a hospital, DSS offices or the DSS Leaflets Unit, PO Box 21, Stanmore, Middlesex HA7 1AY.

The cost of the funeral and burial or cremation is paid out of the deceased's estate. The crematorium fees need to be added to those of the funeral director and any church fees. These will amount to several hundred pounds (about £750 for a simple funeral and cremation in 1991). Where there are no relatives or there is no money in the estate to pay for a funeral the Local Authority or hospital will deal with it.

Probate is obtained where there is a Will whilst Letters of Administration are obtained where there is no Will. Application is made in the way described in Chapter 5. Application is made to the same place in both instances but there are some important differences which are outlined here.

Naturally, where there is in existence a valid Will a deceased person's property will be distributed in accordance with his/her wishes rather than in accordance with the law of intestacy (where there is no Will) under which the dead person did not use the power to dispose of his property as he would wish.

A person who makes a Will can appoint Executors who, if he wishes, can be chosen personally by him so that he will have the satisfaction of knowing that his estate will be well administered by persons in whom he has faith.

At one time, where there was no Will, the persons who administered the deceased Estate, before appointment, were sometimes required to provide an Administration Bond and obtain sureties so as to guarantee the administration of the Estate. However, the procedure has been greatly simplified and now they do not need to produce such Administration Bonds or Sureties. However, in very exceptional circumstances an indemnity guarantee might be required and the Probate Registry or Office will be able to advise you if you fall into this category. Administrators of an Estate where there is no Will take their authority to deal with the Estate from the Grant of Letters of Administration whereas Executors under a Will take their authority to deal with the Estate from the Will itself, and, consequently, may deal with affairs of the deceased person's estate before there has been a Grant of Probate.

Finally, where a person dies seemingly without leaving a Will there arises the problem as to whether there really is a Will or not in existence somewhere. Where a person has made a Will, however, the only real problem that might arise is whether it is a valid Will or whether it has been revoked by some later Will or subsequent marriage.

Who Benefits If There Is No Will?

Where a person dies without leaving a Will their property is disposed of according to the law of intestacy (from the Latin meaning "no Will").

In some circumstances certain persons, such as the surviving spouse, children and other dependants, can claim money from the estate whether there is a Will or not. For such people, even if there is no provision in a Will or there is no Will at all, the Court has wide discretion so as to make provision for them out of the estate if they make a claim. These matters are outside the scope of this book but *everything that is stated in this section on intestacy is still subject to any claims that may be made by these persons*. If any claims of this kind arise, you need legal advice.

Where a person dies without making a Will, or without making a fresh Will having revoked an earlier one, or having married subsequent to making his last Will (unless the Will was clearly made in contemplation of the marriage), then the person's property is disposed of according to what family he leaves. All the property is held by the personal representative so that it can be sold and the proceeds distributed according to the rules that are set out below. The personal representative has the power to postpone the sale. *Personal* items must not be sold unless it is necessary to do so in order to pay for the administration of the estate.

Once the funeral expenses and administration costs have been paid the property is distributed as follows:—

1. If there is a surviving spouse (husband or wife) and there are no children or other descendants, no parents living, no brothers or sisters, or their children living, then the surviving spouse receives all the property absolutely.

2. If there is a surviving spouse (husband or wife) and the estate is valued at less than *£75,000 then the surviving spouse will receive the whole of the estate even if there are other relatives including children. If the estate is over *£75,000 and there are children (whether or not there are any parents, brothers or sisters or their children) then the surviving spouse receives:

   a) all personal items together with

   b) *£75,000 (if that much is available) plus any interest and

   c) a life interest in half the rest of the estate. The other half is given to the children in equal shares absolutely.

A life interest means that the surviving spouse has the right to use it and the income from it for the rest of his/her life but does not have absolute ownership of it. This leaves this half of the estate intact which, after the death of the surviving spouse, is given to the children in equal shares absolutely.

*The figure of £75,000 above (and this applies equally to the figure of £125,000 below) are correct in 1991 but can be changed by Parliament, and sometimes in the past changes have been made to offset the effects of inflation.

3. If there is a surviving spouse (husband or wife) and there are no children and the estate is valued at over *£125,000 then the surviving spouse receives all the estate. If there are parents, brothers or sisters or children of brothers or sisters then the surviving spouse receives:

   a) all personal items together with

   b) *£125,000 (if that much is available) plus any interest and

c) half the residue of the estate absolutely. If there is a parent or parents then the parent(s) receives the other half of the residue absolutely in equal shares. If there is no parent then this half goes to the brothers and sisters in equal shares.

4. If there is no surviving spouse then the estate is held for the children so that all shall have equal shares when they reach the age of 18 or marry, whichever is sooner. But if certain children have been given gifts during the lifetime of the person who has died. then they may find their share cut down by the amount that they have received prior to the person's death.

In this context when dealing with intestacy the word children means and includes illegitimate children and adopted children, so long as there has been a formal adoption order. Children who have been loosely "adopted" without a formal adoption order will not be included. The word children does not include stepchildren and they will receive nothing if a person dies intestate.

5. If there is no surviving spouse and no children then the estate is distributed to all members of one of the following categories in this order:

a) grandchildren, but if none;

b) parents, but if none;

c) brothers and sisters (or their children if the brothers and sisters themselves died before the deceased), but if none;

d) grandparents, but if none;

e) uncles and aunts (or their children if the uncles and aunts themselves died before the deceased).

If all the members of one of these categories have died before the deceased then the estate is distributed in equal shares among the members of the next category.

In all the categories a) to e) where there is more than

one of the persons specified then the residue is shared equally by them, however many there may be.

Children, brothers, sisters, uncles and aunts who die before the date of the death of the person dying intestate are represented by their descendants, so that their share goes to their children.

You will notice that there is no provision for a mistress or co-habitee or common law wife as she is sometimes known, that is, a woman who is living with someone but not married to him. She is not entitled to anything under the law according to intestacy, but she may be able to claim under the Court's discretion for making provision for dependants as set out at the beginning of this Chapter.

Where there has been a divorce the divorced surviving spouse is not entitled to anything under these rules and loses all rights. Divorce dates from the grant of Decree Absolute.

Where two people who are married have been granted an order of judicial separation in the Divorce County Court then, on one of them dying without leaving a Will, the other one will *not* be entitled as the surviving spouse according to the law of intestacy. Yet where two people who are married have been granted an order in the Magistrates Court that they are no longer bound to live with one another then, on one of them dying without leaving a Will, the other one *will* be entitled as a surviving spouse according to the law of intestacy, just like any other surviving spouse.

A surviving spouse has the right to have included as part of his/her entitlement under the above rules any house or flat which is part of the residential estate in which he/she was living at the time of the death. This is so as to ensure that a surviving spouse can stay on in the matrimonial home.

Where children are entitled to receive something under the rules stated above, but have died themselves, then their children are entitled to it whether they are legitimate or illegitimate.

3

The Grant of Probate (or Letters of Administration)

Is grant of Probate or Letters of Administration necessary?

Where the amounts of money and assets in the deceased person's estate are small, it is sometimes possible for you to receive them without having to make an application for a grant of Probate or Letters of Administration.

This will be the case where assets are held by institutions like the Department of National Savings, and Building Societies, but only if the amount which is held in any one of these institutions is not greater than £5,000. It should be stressed that any one of these institutions *can* refuse to make payment until Probate or Letters of Administration have been produced and if there is any difficulty about the deceased person's holding then, most probably, this *will* be required.

Nevertheless, in many cases the institution concerned will make the payment without seeing Probate or Letters of Administration, although it is entirely a matter of discretion. Likewise, although this facility does not extend to money in a bank account or money on a policy which should be paid by an insurance company, in many cases both banks and insurance companies will make payment of small amounts without demanding to see Probate or Letters of Administration.

If the estate of the deceased person is small then you should enquire to see whether payment will be made without Probate or Letters of Administration in which case there is no need for you to make any application for either Probate or Letters of Administration. Where stocks and shares are concerned, even if the amounts are small, a grant of Probate or Letters of Administration probably will be necessary.

To Whom May Letters of Administration Be Granted?

Letters of Administration (where there is no Will) are granted to the person who will administer the estate of the deceased but, of course, it is not anyone who can apply. There is now wide power to have regard to the rights of all persons who are interested in the estate of the deceased person or the proceeds of sale of the estate. Where a person dies without leaving a Will then Grant of Letters of Administration will be made to one or more of the persons who are entitled to receive the deceased's property under the law of intestacy, if they make an application for this purpose. In respect of property put into a settlement by the deceased before his death but where he has left no Will then Letters of Administration as far as that property is concerned will be granted to the trustees of the settlement if they are willing to act. Where a person dies without leaving a Will and the estate is insolvent or there are other special circumstances, then, if the Court thinks it expedient, Letters of Administration may be granted to some other person. Such other person might be a creditor of the insolvent estate. Administration will not be granted to more than four people. Moreover, if the person entitled to the estate is a minor (that is, under the age of eighteen) then administration has to be granted either to a trust corporation or to not less than two individuals.

Grant of Administration Where There Is No Will

Where there is no Will the law states that certain persons will be entitled to have the deceased's estate. The way in which the deceased's estate is divided is dealt with in Chapter 2. This section deals merely with the person(s) to whom the administration of that estate is given. The priority of persons entitled to Grant of Administration is as follows:—

(1) The widow (widower) or, if none;
(2) A child of the dead person (or the children of a child, i.e.
     grandchildren of the dead person, if the child himself/
     herself is dead) or, if none;
(3) A parent of the dead person or, if none;
(4) A brother or sister of the dead person (or, children of
     brothers and sisters if the brothers and sisters themselves
     are dead) or, if none;
(5) Grandparents or, if none;
(6) Uncles and Aunts (or, the children of uncles and aunts if
     the uncles and aunts are dead themselves) or, if none;
(7) The Crown;
(8) Creditors.

Where a Person Dies Leaving a Will But Without
Appointing An Executor

The situation may arise where a person has left a valid Will
but has failed to appoint an Executor in the Will. In such a
circumstance the Court will have to appoint someone to
administer the deceased's estate in accordance with the
provisions of the Will. This is known as a grant of administration "with the Will annexed".

In addition, there are other circumstances in which it will be
necessary for the Court to appoint an administrator by
granting to him/her Letters of Administration with the Will
annexed. These circumstances are as follows:—

(1) Where the Executor has died either before the deceased's
     death or afterwards but having failed to apply for grant;
(2) Where the Executor has renounced his claim for grant;
(3) Where the Executor is under the age of eighteen, a lunatic
     or living outside the United Kingdom. In this case
     administration with the Will annexed is given to another
     person until such time as the executor either reaches the

age of eighteen or ceases to be a lunatic or comes to live within the United Kingdom;

(4) In certain circumstances where the deceased is domiciled abroad but the Will, which appoints an Executor, has not been made in accordance with the law of the land in which the deceased was living;

(5) Where the Will provides for an Executor to deal with the estate after a certain period from the deceased's death but with no appointment of Executor in the meantime;

(6) Where the Will appoints a corporation as Executor other than a trust corporation in which case grant of administration is given to its legal representative.

The function and activity of a person appointed as an administrator in the circumstances outlined above is very similar to that of an Executor.

The Court has wide discretion as to whom it appoints as an administrator in these circumstances but has regard to the rights of all persons who are interested in the estate of the deceased person and may grant administration to a beneficiary under the Will. Such persons, however, have no right as such to be appointed as administrators. Nevertheless, the person who is entitled to the residue of the estate is preferred to the next of kin.

4

Drawing the Estate Together

If you have been named as an Executor in the deceased's Will then, unless you renounce your appointment, you will be responsible for administering the estate. Probably, you will not be the only Executor and it is most important that you should not act in isolation from the other Executors but agree together what should be done.

In many cases the bulk of the work will be done by one Executor but he/she should always obtain the written agreement of the other Executor(s). This might be the situation where a brother and sister are appointed Executors of their father's estate. The brother may well be a businessman and the sister have no business expertise. It is only natural that the brother may well be expected to do most of the work but, nevertheless, he should always obtain the sister's agreement to the actions that he takes in respect of the estate.

If the estate is worth a large amount of money or if it is complicated by settled property to which the dead person was entitled, then the Executor should consult a Solicitor to obtain Probate. Moreover, he should see a Solicitor if there is a problem about tracing persons who are to receive something under the Will, or if the dead person did not leave a Will and there are relatives of whose whereabouts he is not sure.

The object of obtaining Probate is so that the Executor(s) or representatives of the dead person can have the legal authority to deal with the dead person's estate.

The Executor is empowered to deal with the dead person's estate as from the date of death. Grant of Probate merely confirms his powers and is proof to the world. Where there is no Will then you should obtain Letters of Administration (the same procedure as for obtaining Probate) before dealing with the estate.

Valuation of the Estate

Obtain some extra copies of the Death Certificate because, as Executor, you need to enclose these with the letters you have to write. Then the next thing to do is to value the estate.

You will need to get full details of the dead person's estate. You should draw up a list of the property such as house, flat, land, cash, stocks and shares, bank account, savings and including property and amounts that were due on death such as insurance policies. You should have details also of personal property such as car, jewellery, furniture, clothes, etc. You will have to obtain a valuation of these items. On many of the items you can estimate this yourself and there is nothing wrong in doing this so long as you try to make them as accurate as possible.

In the case of the deceased's *Bank Account* you should write to the Bank Manager stating that you are the Executor of the dead person, giving the full name and date of death.

You should ask the Bank Manager the amount of money in the dead person's account together with any other details that might be helpful, such as any securities or valuables that were deposited at the Bank. Moreover, the Bank Manager may be able to tell you the names of any Companies in which the dead person had stocks and shares. The letter to the Bank Manager should ask what steps are necessary in obtaining payment of what is due to the estate.

When writing to the Bank Manager you should ask him to open an Executors' account, although you could ask your own bank or any other to do this. This is the account into which any receipts of the Estate coming in will be paid and from which you will be able to pay out the legacies when you have obtained Probate. Before that happens, however, there may be outstanding debts on the Estate which must be paid such as the telephone and milk bills. If there is cash available in the Estate then you can use this but if not then you should ask the Bank Manager to open a loan account in your name on the security of the Estate from which you can make such payments. This can be converted into the Executors' account in due course. You should not use your existing account or make payments out of your own money.

If you have the Share Certificates or printouts showing shareholdings you will be able to write to the Bank Manager giving details of the stocks and shares and asking him to find out their valuation on the date of the deceased's death.

For an *Insurance Policy* you should write to the Insurance Company stating that you are the Executor of the dead person, giving the full name and date of death, and asking what amount is payable under the Policy.

In the case of a *National Savings Bank Account, National Savings Certificates, S.A.Y.E. contracts, Premium Bonds, British Savings Bonds, Income Bonds or Stock*, you should obtain Form DNS 904 from a Post Office, and send it off as directed. If more than one of the above different types of savings instruments are held, it does not matter since all the different offices will be notified once the Form is sent to the first office.

The purpose of Form DNS 904 is to advise the National Savings of the holder's death, to give the facts to prove that you are entitled to claim the savings and to show whether you wish to keep the money in National Savings (where per-mitted), or to have it repaid. In some instances, National Savings will need to write back to you for more information before the savings can be released.

In the case of money in a *National Savings Bank Account, National Savings Certificates, British Savings Bonds* and

Government Stock on the *National Savings Stock Register* the deceased person, during his/her life, may have allocated such money to another person so that the other person will receive it on the deceased's death. This is a process known as nomination and could be done, up until 1981, by filling in and signing a form obtainable from the Director of Savings. Since 1981 the facility has been withdrawn, but the following rules still apply to any nomination made before 1981. The persons who are so nominated to receive this money, on the deceased's death, can apply to have either the cash or the Certificates/Stock transferred to them by producing the Death Certificate, without having to produce a Grant of Probate or Letters of Administration. Such a nomination takes effect even though it may not be mentioned in the Will.

Obviously, it will not take effect if the person in whose favour the nomination has been made dies before the deceased or, at some time before his death, the deceased revoked the nomination by completing a form of revocation which could be obtained from the same source.

In many cases certain assets, such as a Bank Account, will have been held jointly by the deceased and some other person, such as a joint bank account between husband and wife. Then it is necessary to find the value of the share which belonged to the deceased.

This has to be ascertained with reference to the source of the money. This will determine the proportion of the share of the deceased in the joint asset. Consequently, if a Building Society Account was held jointly by husband and wife but was contributed to entirely by the wife making monthly payments to it out of her savings then, on the death of her husband, he would be regarded as having no share in the account even though he could have drawn upon it during his lifetime.

If, however, it was the wife who had died then the whole of the Building Society Account would come into the valuation of her estate upon her death. It will not always be that simple, though, and the shares have to be ascertained by reference to contributions made over a period of time. In the example of the Building Society, if the husband had contributed £3,000 over the years and the wife had contributed £2,000 over the years then the proportionate share of the husband would be 3/5ths. Thus, if on the date of death of the husband, there was £500 in the Building Society Account the valuation for the purposes of the estate of the dead husband would be £300.

It is important to draw the distinction between ascertaining the shares for the purposes of valuation for taxation on death and entitlement to the joint asset. With any joint asset, whether it be a Bank Account or land or other asset, the rule is that the deceased's share passes automatically to the other person. In the case of the joint Building Society Account, on the death of her husband, the valuation of his estate for taxation purposes will include the £300 mentioned above but the whole of the Account, including this money, will pass to his wife who will have the absolute right to it, so that the £300 does not form part of the estate which can be distributed to other beneficiaries. The same principle applies with a house which, if held in joint names, means that on the death of the husband the wife is entitled to the whole of the house including the husband's share since as a joint owner this passes to her automatically. The husband is not entitled to dispose of his share of the house in any other way in his Will.

In the case of the *house* or *flat* you will need to assess its market value as at the date of death and you are entitled to take into account that it would have to be sold quickly and in its present state. Although, ultimately, the District Valuer will check the value of the property there is nothing wrong in estimating this yourself initially. Since this valuation is for the purposes of payment of Inheritance Tax it is probably better to estimate on the low rather than the high side. The actual value of the property has to be reduced by the amount of any outstanding Mortgage. If there is a Mortgage you should write to the Mortgagee (the Building Society, Local Authority or someone else, as the case may be) stating the full name of the deceased and the date of death, together with the name of the property and, preferably, the reference number of the Mortgage and asking for the amount of the Mortgage outstanding on the date of death.

In the case of a property owned jointly by the deceased and a survivor, such as his wife, the amount attributable to the deceased's estate for valuation purposes is the amount of the total valuation of the property, less the Mortgage outstanding, and divided by two where there are two joint owners.

Although this is the most common form of joint ownership there is another form of joint ownership known as a tenancy in common. This means that the persons who are the joint owners have clearly identifiable shares in the property, not necessarily of equal proportions. Unlike a joint ownership where, on the death of one person, that person's share passes automatically to the other(s), in the case of a tenancy in common if one of the joint owners dies then his/her share does not pass automatically to the others but becomes part of the estate and can pass to a beneficiary either under directions contained in the Will or, if there is no Will, under the laws of intestacy, in other words, to a descendant.

The question of whether joint ownership of a property is the unseverable kind, or a tenancy in common, can be ascertained from the actual deeds of the property but, if you have any doubt, then it would be wise to consult a Solicitor. If the ownership is a tenancy in common then you will have to know the proportion of the property that was held by the deceased in order that you can enter this as a valuation in the deceased's estate.

If there is any *pension* fund or other money to which the

dead person is entitled then you should write to the employers or institutions stating the same information as to the Bank Manager and asking for full details.

There are many pension schemes which entitle a dead person's widow to receive an income following her husband's death. This should be clarified with the deceased's employers. The dead person's estate will be entitled to receive any pension due to the deceased up to the actual day of his death, and his employers should be asked to work out the amount that has to be paid to the estate. You should also enquire of the employers whether any capital sum is due to be paid to the estate under the pension scheme, either by way of return of contributions paid by the deceased if he died before retirement age and/or a further lump amount. A point to watch here is that, in some cases, such lump amount can be paid to the deceased's widow, children or other person. Naturally, if this is the case then the amount will not form part of the estate for valuation purposes. It will have to be taken into account only if it is paid to the estate.

If he/she was of pensionable age the deceased probably was receiving a state retirement pension. When the death is registered you will receive not only a Certificate for Burial or Cremation (no charge) and a Death Certificate (a small fee) which you will need for the estate but also a Certificate of Registration of Death (no fee) which is for use only for Social Security claims. You should answer the questions on the back and send it together with the deceased's pension book to your local DSS office which will pay to the deceased's estate any pension owing up to the date of death. One of these questions asks if the deceased's widow wants to claim widow's benefit (she does not have to be of pensionable age). Widows/widowers in receipt of retirement pension may be entitled to extra pension based on the deceased's national insurance contribution record. See Appendix.

You should list any money that was owed to the dead person which he/she should have received had he/she not died. This will include personal loans that were made during his/her lifetime by him/her to other people.

You should now make a list of all the *debts* that the dead person owed because these will have to be paid out of the estate. These are not just loans that the dead person might have received during his/her lifetime but include all bills, overdrafts, hire/purchase liabilities, credit card accounts, etc. You will have to check on these things and may have to contact shops and other places where the dead person may have had an account.

If there is any doubt about the extent of the debts then you can advertise in the London Gazette and a newspaper which circulates in the area in which the estate is situated although, in addition, you must do all you can to bring the dead person's death to the attention of any possible creditors about whose existence you may be aware. The advertisement advises creditors that they must submit claims by a certain date, after which you can distribute the estate having obtained Probate. Even if a creditor fails to make a claim within the time specified in the advertisement he can still do so, but it will be made against the beneficiaries to whom the estate has been distributed and not against you as Executor who will be protected. The date by which claims have to be submitted which is stated in the advertisement has to be a minimum of two months from the date on which the advertisement appears in the newspapers.

One debt for which the estate may be liable and about which you may have no knowledge is if the dead person gave a guarantee to another person during his/her lifetime. Hopefully, if this is the case, the person making the Will would have foreseen the difficulty for his/her Executor and will have left a clear note near or with the Will to the effect that he/she did give a guarantee. If so, then this is something that you must bear in mind as a possible claim on the estate.

Once the funeral has taken place you should ask the funeral directors for their account so as to know the exact amount of the *funeral expenses.*

Personal items will have to be valued, but this need not be done for every individual piece. An overall value is sufficient for all the items, although this should be as accurate as possible. Mostly, an idea of the value can be obtained by looking at the prices of similar second-hand goods in shops. As far as vehicles are concerned, such as a car, there is available from most bookshops at least one publication which is a monthly motorist's guide to used car prices. It is important to remember that the valuation should be what the items were worth at the date of death. You must also list any cash that was left by the deceased.

Finally you should write to the local Inspector of Taxes to see if there is any *income tax* liability of the dead person or whether the estate is entitled to any tax refund. If the deceased was self-employed and/or had income from investments then almost certainly there will be a tax liability, since he will not have paid tax on his receipts (other than on dividends and bank and building society interest from which tax has been deducted at source) for the period from the beginning of this tax year to the date of his death.

If, however, he was in employment and tax was deducted from his salary or wages under the P.A.Y.E. system then there may well be a tax refund due to his estate. This is especially likely if the person died shortly after the beginning of the tax year (April) since he is still entitled to receive the personal tax allowance for the whole year although he will be taxed only on the income up to his date of death, which may be less than the allowance.

5

Probate Application

Where To Get The Forms

Where there is a Will in existence a sole Executor appointed by the Will will obtain Probate. If there are two or several Executors then it is not necessary for all of them to obtain Probate as the application can be made by any one of the Executors. Where there is no Will then the application is for Grant of Letters of Administration and is made by the next of kin of the deceased as explained on page 33.

Firstly, you must obtain the necessary forms. This can be done by writing to or telephoning:

The Probate Personal Application Department,
Principal Registry of the Family Division,
2nd Floor, Somerset House
Strand
London WC2R 1LP
Telephone: 071-936-6983

Personal enquiries should be made in Room 83.

The Department is open from 10.00 a.m. to 4.30 p.m. from Monday to Friday but is closed on Saturday.

Alternatively, you can apply to a Local District Probate Registry or Sub-Registry open from 9.30 a.m. to 4.00 p.m. Monday to Friday, closed on Saturday. Addresses of these are given in Appendix II.

Application in person, though not by post or telephone, can also be made at one of the local Probate Offices, which are part-time only. The towns in which they are situated are shown in Appendix II. You should not write, send forms to, or telephone the Probate Offices. All communications should be sent or telephoned to the Principal Registry, or to the appropriate Registry or Sub-Registry. The local Probate Offices are only open at certain times of day and perhaps only on one day a week, or even as little as one or two days a month. If you are calling without appointment, confirm the days and times of opening in advance.

Filling In The Probate Forms

You obtain from the local Probate Registry or Probate Office a brown envelope containing the following:

1. Probate application form (Form PA1 — blue and white);
2. A Return of the Whole Estate (Form Cap 44 — blue);
3. Inland Revenue Capital Taxes Office Schedule of Real, Leasehold Heritable and Immoveable Property (Form Cap 37 — yellow and white);
4. Inland Revenue Capital Taxes Office Schedule of stocks and shares etc (Form Cap 40);
5. Form PA5 Spouse's contributions — white.

With these forms comes a blue booklet "How to obtain probate — a guide to the applicant acting without a solicitor" (Form PA2) together with sheets giving office addresses and fees. You should read the blue booklet carefully. You may find that a grant of probate is not needed at all.

Complete the forms legibly, preferably in capital letters (this is required for Form PA1). Don't send in the forms until you have full details of the assets and liabilities, but if there is any difficulty in finding out the nature or value of any particular item, or doubt as to how any part of the forms should be completed, then they can be sent in, completed as far as possible with a note explaining the difficulty.

Form PA1

This form opens out and has six sides. You should complete only the white sections. It must be done in capital letters.

Section 1. Write in the name of the Probate Registry or local office at which you wish to be interviewed. Select the one which is easiest for you to attend. A list of these is given in the blue booklet. You must be interviewed (usually only one interview is required) at one of the Registries or local offices.

Section 2. You must give the forenames and surname of the person who has died as well as listing any assets which were held in another name and giving the other name(s). You must give the deceased's occupation (or 'retired') and tick the box for marital status.

Section 3. You have to state if there is a Will and list those executors who are not applying for probate.

Section 4. List the number of relatives of the deceased in each category of relationship and stating how many are 18 years or over and how many are under 18. There are further questions about the deceased.

Section 5. This is where you complete details about yourself as the person applying for probate.

Finally, there is a reminder at the bottom of this page that you must send in with the form: 1) the death certificate, 2) the *original* Will (if there is one), and 3) the account of the estate (Form Cap 44).

Form PA5

This form should be completed only if the deceased left a surviving spouse and there is a matrimonial home in the *sole* name of the deceased.

Form Cap 44

This form consists of eight numbered pages but its size should not frighten you. This is the one for which you have compiled lists of the deceased's property and valuations, and debts. If you have any problems or worries about some of the questions then you should ask about them. Many of them require only a tick in a box marked YES or NO.

Section 1. Schedule of Assets. This requires you to list assets of the deceased in the United Kingdom. The assets to be listed here are everything owned by the deceased or due to the deceased from any source at the date of death. It includes items or money due to the deceased even if they have not yet been received. You have to put the value against all the different categories of assets listed and if there are some for which there is no category then these should be listed separately on a different sheet of paper and the total value of them entered at item 12 with a note against it "see separate list". You should attach the list to the form. Against Question 1 'Cash' you should put all the cash that is found at home and elsewhere other than in the bank. Against Question 8 'Other stocks, shares or investments, including unit trust' you should put the total value but also complete Form Cap 40. Likewise, against Question 15 'Freehold and leasehold property (houses, flats, land etc)' you should put the total value but also complete Form Cap 37.

You will remember the different types of joint ownership (see page 41). If any property was owned jointly by the deceased and some other person and passes under the Will to another then it should be entered under this section. If, however, it passes to the other joint owner by survivorship then it should be entered under Question 1 on page 5 and not Section 1.

There then follows a section 'Schedule of debts due to persons resident in the United Kingdom' the first of which is funeral expenses. The cost of the funeral is taken out of the overall value of the estate before any liability to Inheritance Tax is considered. Under this heading you should also include any bills, overdrafts, store accounts still owing, electricity and gas bills etc. You will need to contact the local authority, water authority, electricity and gas boards so as to have them itemise the amounts owing up to the date of death. Read the meters in the deceased's house as soon as possible after death. Don't list here either mortgage or business debts.

Section 2 deals with any assets and debts outside the United Kingdom.

The bottom half of page 5 and over to page 6 deals with joint assets which pass by survivorship. There is Question 2 about nominated assets (see page 39) whereby the deceased could, up till 1981, nominate persons to receive certain assets on his/her death.

Question 3 is about substantial gifts and other transfers made during the deceased's lifetime and sets out those which need not be disclosed. Small gifts need not be detailed. Gifts made before seven years from the date of death need not be disclosed. Finally, do not forget to sign the declaration at the bottom of page 8.

Form Cap 37

This is a Schedule of Real and Leasehold/immovable Property, in other words, any land or buildings belonging to the deceased or in which he had an interest. It should be noted that separate forms are required to be used for properties in (1) England and Wales. (2) Scotland. (3) Northern Ireland or (4) outside the U.K. At the top of the form the name and date of death of the deceased must be entered. In column 2 you should put the description of the property, e.g. "1, Whiteacre, Blacktown in the County of Greenshire". In column 3 is placed either "freehold" or "leasehold". In column 4 any tenancies of the property, together with details of the tenant, period of tenancy, rent and landlord's outgoings, are entered. In column 5 you should enter any agricultural part: this is because agricultural land is given certain relief from Inheritance Tax. The value of the property must be placed in column 6: either your own estimate, that of an estate agent, or that of the District Valuer. If it is that of the District Valuer then this should be indicated as well as any sales of property, with the sale price and completion date if any property is on the market to be sold.

Form Cap 40

This is the Statement of Stocks and Shares. Enter the name of the dead person and the date of death at the top. In this form you should list all the stocks and shares and securities owned by the deceased, putting first those which are quoted on the London Stock Exchange. The first column is for the general description, e.g. "Treasury $5\frac{1}{2}$% 08/12". This includes the unit of share e.g. £1 if they are £1 shares. The second column is for the number of shares or the financial amount of stock held, so that if the deceased had 100 £1 shares this should be written as 100. The next column is for the market price at the date of valuation which is the date of death of the deceased. This can be discovered by asking the Bank Manager or a Stockbroker. Alternatively, you can find this out yourself by purchasing a copy of the London Stock Exchange Official List for the date of the death, by writing to the Council of the Stock Exchange, Official List Office, London EC2N 1HP. They can advise the fee for this. All the shares quoted on the London Stock Exchange are included in this publication and against each one there are two prices. The market price which should be entered in Form 40 is a quarter up from the lower to the higher, so that if the two prices quoted were 80p and 84p then the market price would be 81p. If the source of the market price is other than the Stock Exchange List for the date of valuation, details should be given in Column 3 or in a separate schedule. This might apply to shares in a private company since these are not quoted on the Stock Exchange. (The valuation of shares in Private Companies is a complex matter about which you should consult a solicitor.)

The final column asks for the principal value which is merely the total amount that the shares are worth at the market price, in other words the market price multiplied by the number of shares held.

Sending Off The Probate Forms

You should try to fill in the Probate Forms as best you can, but if you have difficulty in finding out the nature of any particular item or are in doubt as to how any part of the forms should be completed, you can still send in the forms completed as far as possible with a note explaining your difficulty.

You should make sure that you send or deliver the following documents:
(1) Completed forms PA1, Cap 44, Cap 37, Cap 40, and PA5;
(2) The Death Certificate;
(3) The Will (keeping a photocopy in case the original is lost in the post);
(4) A covering letter stating whether you want to go for interview at either the Probate Registry or the Probate Office, whichever is more convenient. You should state any date or time of the day that is inconvenient or at which you cannot attend. An appointment will then be made, but it can be only during the working hours of the Probate Registry or the Probate Office.

You can deliver the above documents to the Probate

Registry or the local office at the address at the top of Form PA1 during office hours or, alternatively, using the addressed envelope in which the forms arrived, you can send the above documents to that address. It is preferable to send them by registered post. If you deliver them personally you can ask to be interviewed on the same day if this is possible. Remember that all documents must be sent to a Probate Registry and *NOT* to a local Probate Office.

The Appointment at the Probate Office

Once the forms have been sent/delivered you will receive notice of the appointment time, date and place.

The people in the Probate Registries and Probate Offices are used to dealing with personal applications by ordinary people, so there need be no fear of going to ask questions. The staff are both sympathetic and helpful. It is useful if you take along with you all the papers and notes that you have amassed since these may help you to answer any questions.

The appointment is to iron out any problems and to get you to swear and sign a form that the information you have given is true to the best of your knowledge. This is Cap 200 if the estate is worth more than the current threshold for Inheritance Tax and Cap 202 if it is just under. Within three or four weeks you will receive back, by post, all the relevant completed forms which are required for the Grant of Probate.

Small Estates

Most of the estates are below the threshold for payment of Inheritance Tax and none is payable. Where Inheritance Tax is payable, however, a grant of Probate will not be issued until tax has been paid. This involves the preparation of an account for the estate which is sent after your interview to the Capital Taxes Office which assesses how much tax needs to be paid. An account is not required, however, if the total value of the estate is well below the threshold, consists only of property which has passed under the deceased's Will or the rules of intestacy, any property outside the UK is below £15,000 and the deceased died domiciled in the UK and had made no lifetime gifts chargeable to Inheritance Tax. But the Capital Taxes Office can, if it wishes, still ask for an account within thirty-five days.

Probate Fees

You should remember that you will have to pay the probate fees, which are set out in the Appendix, at the time of the appointment at the probate office or registry before probate can be granted, so you should come prepared. Any Inheritance Tax payable must be paid before probate is granted and you should read Chapter 11 to see the various ways in which the money for this can be raised.

When Someone Dies Abroad

It should be remembered that the object of obtaining Probate is so that a person can deal with the estate and property of the deceased in the country in which it is situated. Consequently, if a person dies abroad and all his property is situated in that country abroad then it is necessary only to apply for Grant of Probate in that country in order to be able to deal with his estate. In such circumstances the Grant of Probate will be governed by the law of that particular country. The situation may arise, however, in which a person dies abroad but has part of his property or estate situated in this country. In this case it is advisable that you should seek the help of a Solicitor.

The relevant factor to remember, however, is the domicile of the person who dies abroad. Domicile means where a person has his permanent home. Consequently, if a person dies abroad on holiday but has his permanent home in

England then probate should be taken out in England so as to be able to deal with his estate in this country. If a person who dies has his home in England then a Grant of Probate in England is good for dealing with all his property in the United Kingdom whether in Northern Ireland, Scotland or Wales, as well as England.

If a person is domiciled abroad, e.g. has his permanent home abroad, but has property or estate in this country, however, then it will be necessary to apply for a Grant of Probate in this country. The requirement here will be to show that the deceased person's Will is valid in order that probate may be granted here. If the Court of the foreign country has declared the Will to be valid then it will be recognised in this country as valid on production of a duly authenticated copy of the Will together with evidence of the Court's decision, usually a copy of its decree under the seal of the Court. A translation of both the documents will have to accompany them and, unless the translator has an official position then he must file an affidavit giving his qualification and confirming that the translation is accurate.

Alternatively, probate will be granted in this country if proof is given that the deceased person's Will is valid under the law of the country in which he was resident at the time of his death. This proof can be provided by an affidavit sworn by a lawyer or other expert in the law of the country in which the person died stating that the Will is valid under the law of that country. Such a person could be the Ambassador of the particular country.

6
Administering the Estate

Once you have obtained Probate you are now in a position to distribute the estate to the beneficiaries according to the terms of the Will. There may still be tax to be paid or the uncertainty of any late creditors' claims or other debts of the estate which might arise. In such circumstances you may feel that it is prudent not to distribute all the estate but to keep some back for the time being in order to meet such eventualities. This is known as a partial distribution. It is fairly easy where there is a substantial residue to be split up between one or two close relatives of the deceased. Indeed, you may be the only or one of such beneficiaries of the residue. This means that you can pay out the pecuniary legacies and gifts to charities and transfer over to the beneficiaries specific items left to them under the Will.

Keeping a Record

You should keep a careful record of all the amounts that you distribute according to the terms of the Will. Where there are specific gifts to charities or other bodies or individuals you should obtain a receipt and keep this. Indeed, you should keep all records for a period of twelve years. You will need also to keep a careful record of all amounts that are paid into the estate between the date of death and final distribution. These will be items such as dividends and interest payable to the estate on the deceased's shareholdings before you have transferred them to the beneficiaries under the Will or sold them in order to make payments in cash. This income may be subject to income tax and you should keep all the vouchers showing deduction of tax at the standard rate at source which will accompany such payments. There may be repayment of income tax due to the estate if the deceased died during the tax year and was paid through the PAYE system.

Shares

Some of these may have to be sold in order to pay pecuniary legacies and this can be done through a bank or stockbroker who may charge less. Other shares can be transferred to beneficiaries under the Will. In both cases the company's registrar will need to see a sealed copy of the probate and will send a stock transfer form which you can complete, filling in the name of the person to whom the shares are to be transferred.

On the back of the stock transfer form is a section about stamp duty. Stamp duty will be abolished altogether for share transactions once the International Stock Exchange has introduced "paperless dealing", that is doing away with share certificates. Shares which are transferred into the name of a beneficiary named in a Will, however, are exempt in any event. You should write in this section "I hereby certify that this instrument falls within category . . . in the Schedule to the Stamp Duty (Exempt Instruments) Regulations 1987". The category you fill in will depend on the transaction:

Category B is where the property is the subject of a specific legacy to the beneficiary named in the Will (or his nominee);

Category C is where the transfer is from an intestate's estate to the person entitled on intestacy;

Category D is where shares are used to satisfy a pecuniary legacy; and

Category E is where the transfer is of shares part of the residuary estate to the beneficiary under the Will.

Where shares are held on behalf of the deceased by a broker

A Protective Trust can be made for a shorter period, such as:

"I bequeath £10,000 to my son Harold upon Protective Trust until he reach the age of 25."

This would mean that if he does not become bankrupt before 25 Harold would have the income from the £10,000 until he reached 25. The £10,000, would then be divided up among himself, wife and children, if he has any, at the discretion of the Trustees.

If Harold becomes bankrupt before the age of 25, he loses his absolute entitlement to the money and the £10,000 may be divided up at the Trustees' discretion among his wife and children, if he has any, or among those who would be entitled to his property on his death if he has neither wife nor children. Thus, as a Trustee, you may find yourself in a position exercising considerable discretion.

Persons Not Allowed to Benefit

There are some persons who are not allowed to benefit from a provision in a Will even though the deceased person may have made specific gifts to such persons. Broadly, the following persons are unable to benefit from the Will:—

1. Witnesses to the Will and their spouses and persons claiming under them. The signature of the person making the Will has to be witnessed by two persons (unless the person making the Will is a Serviceman on active duty). Those two people are not allowed to take any gift under the terms of the Will and, if there is a gift to a person who has acted as a Witness to the signature or to his/her wife/husband then that gift fails and it becomes part of the residuary estate of the person making the Will.

   This only applies to gifts which are meant for the Witnesses or their spouses. Thus it would not apply to a

gift of property to Arthur Bloggins for him to hold it on
Trust for the benefit of Baby Bloggins. The gift would
not fail, although Arthur Bloggins had witnessed the
signature, because the gift was not for himself but was
for Baby Bloggins.

A person who witnesses the signature on a codicil to
the Will, however, will be able to receive a gift of
property under a term in the Will itself so long as he does
not receive anything under the terms of the codicil.

So long as there are two persons who have witnessed
the signature to a Will and who do not receive any gifts in
it then it does not matter if other people who do receive
gifts in the Will also witness the signature. These people
will still be able to receive the gifts, even though they
witnessed the signature, so long as there are also two
witnesses who or whose spouses do not receive any gifts.

2. Killing the person making the Will. It used to be the law
that under no circumstances could a person who had
unlawfully killed, or aided or abetted or procured the
death of, the person making the Will benefit from its
provisions. This is called the "forfeiture rule" but has
now been modified. Where the forfeiture rule would
otherwise preclude a person from receiving any property
under a Will then the court can make an order allowing
a person to receive the property if it considers that, in the
circumstances, the justice of the case demands it. This
might apply, for example, where a person is convicted of
manslaughter of the testator, or killing him in a car
crash where there was no intention to harm or kill him.
Such an application to the court, however, must be
made within three months of the conviction. This does
not apply, however, to a murderer. Where a person is
convicted of the murder of the testator then the
forfeiture rule takes effect without any possible modifica-

tion and he can receive nothing under the Will. The forfeiture rule does not preclude anyone from making a claim under the Inheritance (Provision for Family and Dependants) Act 1975. Any claims of this kind mean you need a solicitor's help.

3. Fraud, fear, coercion and excessive pestering. If it can be shown that a beneficiary, (that is someone who is entitled to receive a gift of money or property under the terms of the Will) has induced the Testator (that is, the person making the Will) to include the provision for his/her benefit by fraud, fear, or coercion, or excessive pestering then he/she will not be able to receive any of the gift.

Fraud arises in the situation where someone wants a person to make a provision in a Will and who tells that person a lie. For fraud to be established the person making the statement must know what he is doing and must know that it is a lie (or not care whether it is a lie or not). He must intend the person making the Will to act upon the lie and the person making the Will must actually do so.

Thus, if Mr. Bloggins tells his wife a lie with a view to her leaving him some more money in her Will, and she actually does so, then that provision in the Will may be invalidated. Similarly, if Mrs. Bloggins threatens her husband with a carving knife and stands over him whilst he makes his Will, or if she nags him about it every morning before breakfast, the provisions may be invalidated.

This, however, differs from excessive flattery or influence which falls short of coercion. In these situations the Will is valid: it only comes into question when there is undue influence involving coercion.

In one case a man who was suffering from Parkinson's

Disease drew up his Will only six days before he died. The Will was set aside on the grounds that he did not know or approve of the contents of the Will and was acting under the undue influence of his wife. It was said by the Judge that the Will of an old and infirm person ought to be witnessed by a Doctor who satisfies himself that the person making the Will is capable of doing so and understands what is written in the Will. The Doctor should make a record of his examination and findings.

4. Gifts for purposes which go on forever. Where a gift is non-charitable then the Law will not uphold it if it is likely to go on forever. For example, if a provision in a Will left the sum of £10,000 to be held on Trust and the income used to paint the deceased person's front door every year, then in the absence of a limit of the number of years that this should go on it could go on forever. The Law will normally not allow this, since it is felt that there should be a time in the foreseeable future when the £10,000 should be used.

Ambiguity in the Will

The Court now has wide powers to make a Will accord with the intentions of the person who made it if it fails to do so as a result of a clerical error or a failure to understand his instructions. This is called rectifying the Will and consists of altering the wording so that it has the effect of according with the testator's intentions. It involves an application to the Court but, except with the Court's permission, this must be made within six months of the date on which probate is first taken out. So if the Will is ambiguous or misleading it is not necessarily a disaster from the testator's point of view. The personal representatives or executors are not held liable for having distributed any part of the estate after the end of six months from the date on which probate is first taken out if it turns out that such a distribution was not the intention of the testator. The beneficiaries, the people who receive such a distribution, however, should beware! The Court can recover any property distributed if it decides to rectify the Will. If any part of the Will is meaningless or the language is ambiguous in itself or in the light of surrounding circumstances then the Court will look at the surrounding evidence, including evidence of the testator's intention, in order to interpret the Will. This is where any letters of the deceased testator or any recollection of anything he/she may have said on the subject could be important and certainly should not be destroyed, lost, or forgotten.

One further matter should be mentioned in respect of a Will that is not quite clear. Where the Will devises or bequeaths property to the testator's spouse in absolute terms but also tries to leave an interest in the same property to the testator's children then the spouse takes the property absolutely despite the attempted gift to the children.

8

Trustees

If you have been appointed a Trustee under the terms of a Will then you would be well advised to consult a solicitor if the provisions are complicated. Nevertheless, the administration of a Trust set up under a Will can be a simple matter if there are only one or a few beneficiaries, that is, persons who are entitled to benefit from the Trust. If you have been appointed a Trustee you cannot be compelled to accept the office.

Having accepted, however, you are responsible for the property that is placed into the Trust fund.

You should ensure that there is a proper inventory of all the Trust property. If, for example, you are Trustee of a settlement which enables a surviving spouse to stay in a property for the rest of his/her life and there are goods in the property that form part of the Trust then you should make sure that the inventory is signed by the surviving spouse who occupies the property. Some trusts give a duty or a power to the Trustees to invest money in the Trust fund. Details of this may be given in the Will which may include the purchase of land and property. The scope of investments in stocks and shares and other securities is governed by the Trustee Investments Act, 1961 which sets out the securities in which Trustees are authorised to invest. If the Will directs and requires Trustees to make an investment in some specific way then they are under a duty to invest in that way even though it may be a bad investment and may cause a loss to the Trust Fund. Even where it is not expressly stated in the Will that the Trustees can vary the investments there is a general power to change investments so long as they come within the provisions of the Trustee Investments Act, 1961. The Trustee can invest any of the property in the Trust Fund.

subject to the provisions of the Will, in what are known as "narrower-range" investments. These include National Savings Certificates, Deposits in the Post Office Savings Bank, Government Fixed-Interest Securities, Public or Local Authority Fixed-Interest Securities and others, full details of which can be found in the Act or from a solicitor.

In exercising the duty or power of investment the Trustee must choose only investments which are within the terms of the Trust or the Trustee Investments Act and must use the care and caution which an ordinary man of business, regardful of the pecuniary interests in the future of those having claims upon him, would exercise in the management of his own property.

Where there is more than one beneficiary the Trustee has a duty to act impartially between them and in accordance with the provisions of the Will. The point to remember is that a Trustee must carry out the directions contained in the Will, since not to do is a breach of trust. The only way in which this can be avoided is if all the beneficiaries join together and agree to a course of action in respect of the Trust Fund or Property which would otherwise be a breach of trust. Consequently, all the beneficiaries acting together (provided there are no other potential beneficiaries) can defeat the terms of a Trust Fund set up by a Will. In addition, there are certain circumstances where the directions about a Trust Fund can be altered if a Court makes an order.

As the name implies, a Trustee is in a position of trust and, therefore, unless directions contained in the Will expressly provide otherwise, a Trustee is not allowed to make a profit nor to put himself in a position where his interest and duty conflict. This means that unless there is a provision in the Will for specific payment of the Trustee then you, as Trustee, will receive no remuneration for the work that you do in connection with the Trust.

Payment of the Trustee may be authorised, however, by the provisions of the Will or, in certain circumstances, the Court can order payment. It is possible for a Trustee to appoint an agent to carry out the work on his/her behalf but the Trustee will be responsible for that agent's actions if the Trustee has failed properly to supervise the agent. There should be two or more Trustees, but each is accountable only for his own acts, receipts, neglects or defaults and not for those of any other Trustee unless this has been caused through his own wilful default. (It was formerly the law that a Trustee would be liable for a breach of trust arising through the act or default of his co-Trustee if he merely left a matter in the hands of his co-Trustee without enquiry.)

Essentially the law means that the Trustee must take proper care of the Trust Funds and of the way in which he deals with them.

It is also the responsibility of the Trustee to make sure that the beneficiaries who are meant to receive the income or trust property actually receive it themselves and that it does not go to anyone else. In order to safeguard himself a Trustee should keep proper Accounts.

Although the Trustee must not receive any remuneration for his work unless it is specifically authorised by the terms of the Trust he is entitled to receive repayment for costs and expenses incurred in the administration of the Trust.

Any Trustee must look carefully at the provisions of the Trust to see exactly what he can/cannot do. In many cases the Trustee will have a power to sell part or all of the Trust property and to pay over to the beneficiaries either the income from the Trust property, or both the income and part of the capital which may amount to the whole if this is authorised by the terms of the Trust.

Failure to carry out the duties properly, or acting against the terms of the Trust, constitutes a breach of trust for which the Trustee is liable to the beneficiaries. Consequently, if a loss is made by a Trustee acting outside the terms of the Trust he will be responsible to the beneficiaries to make good that loss.

9
Charities and Other Special Cases

Charitable Purposes

The Law relating to charities is far from simple and it is quite complicated sometimes to try to establish whether a certain institution or purpose is charitable or not. Consequently, if you find yourself as a Trustee with a discretion to make gifts to charity then you might well feel it advisable to consult a solicitor so as to ascertain whether a particular institution or body to which you intend to make a gift out of the estate is charitable or not. It is a question of law whether something is charitable or not, and this has often come before the Courts to decide. They are guided by the fact that in order to be charitable a gift must be for the benefit of the community or of an appreciably important class of the community. An old Act of Parliament in Queen Elizabeth I's time gives an idea of what matters can be regarded as charitable:—

> "The relief of aged, impotent and poor people; the maintenance off sick and maimed soldiers and mariners, schools of learning, free schools and scholars in universities; the repair of bridges, ports, havens, causeways, churches, seabanks and highways; the education and preferment of orphans; the relief, stock or maintenance for houses of correction; the marriages of poor maids, the supporting, aid and help of young tradesmen, handicraftsmen and persons decayed; the relief or redemption of prisoners or captives; and aid or ease of any poor inhabitant, etc."

In a case during the last century a Judge said that the idea of charity could be classified into four divisions:

1. Relief of poverty;
2. Advancement of education;
3. Advancement of religion:
4. Other purposes beneficial to the community not falling under any of the other heads.

If in a Will a specific gift is made to a particular charity and that charity has ceased to exist by the date of the deceased person's death then the gift will merely become part of the residue of the estate and will lose its exemption from Inheritance Tax. This difficulty can be avoided, however, if, in the Will, a general charitable intention was expressed which might be set out as follows:

> "I bequeath the sum of £5,000 to ABC Charity. For the avoidance of doubt I desire that this sum of £5,000 be applied for charitable purposes."

In this situation if the ABC Charity has ceased to exist by the time of the deceased person's death then it will be a matter for you the Executor to apply the £5,000 to some other charity as close in object as possible to the original one. It has been decided by the Courts that a gift for the "Maintenance and benefit of any relatives of mine whom my Trustees shall consider to be in special need" was a charitable trust. Furthermore, there is nothing to restrict this to relatives living at the date of death. Consequently, it could apply to relatives who were born after the date of death. When one remembers the important fact that gifts to charities are exempt from Inheritance Tax this may be a way of benefiting relatives while avoiding tax. The discretion as to which relatives should be beneficiaries would be left to the Trustees and a clause in a Will giving effect to this might be as follows:

> "I bequeath the sum of £500 to A and B to be held on Trust for the maintenance and benefit of any relatives of mine whom my Trustees shall consider to be in special need and poverty."

Gifts to Animals which are Charitable Gifts

Gifts to particular animals, such as a pet dog or cat, are not considered to be charitable. Gifts to animals in general, or a species of animal, can be charitable. The test of whether such a gift is charitable or not is not whether it benefits the animals concerned but whether it benefits mankind. This can be by encouraging a more humane attitude towards animals, but, of course, it can be also by assisting mankind in research. A gift will not be considered to be charitable if the overall object does not assist mankind.

Consequently, a gift on trust or to a charity whose objects are the prevention of cruelty to animals, such as the R.S.P.C.A., to relieve suffering in animals, such as the P.D.S.A., will be charitable. A gift for the abolition of experiments on animals or to an anti-vivisection society, however, will not be charitable since this would in law be considered to hinder medical research and would not be to the overall benefit of mankind.

Gifts and Racial Discrimination

The legislation dealing with racial discrimination applies to Wills but will not affect any charities whose objects are to benefit people of a certain nationality or ethnic origin, etc. Consequently, discrimination in making a gift to a charity for persons who are of a particular ethnic group or race will be lawful. Discrimination *against* people, however, as opposed to discrimination *for* people, is unlawful: it would be unlawful to make a gift to a charity for persons of all races except a particular one.

The situation can be summarised by example:

A gift in trust for the benefit of disabled Jews would be lawful discrimination and allowed.

A gift in trust for the benefit of disabled persons except disabled Jews would be unlawful discrimination and disallowed.

Clubs and Company Employees

A gift to the members of a club who are in poverty is charitable.

A gift to the employees of a company is not charitable unless it is for poor employees.

Gifts to the Aged

A gift for the benefit of the aged is charitable even if there is no mention of poverty. Thus, providing a sheltered home or a day centre or luncheon club for the aged will all be charitable gifts.

Gifts to the Disabled

Likewise, a gift for the benefit of the disabled or incapacitated is charitable even if there is no mention of poverty. This will include gifts to the physically handicapped, the blind, the deaf and dumb, the war disabled and any purpose connected with them such as the provision of a nursing home.

Gifts for the Relief of Poverty

A gift is charitable if it is for the relief of poverty, and this includes words such as destitute, needy, deserving, special need, distress and phrases such as "falling on evil days". Poverty does not mean the bread line. It is a relative term and, consequently, can include people who have moderate means. A gift for the relief of poverty can be charitable if it is only for a certain section of the community and does not have to be for the community as a whole. The following gifts are charitable:—

To the poor persons of a particular town or village.

To the poor persons of a club.

To the poor persons of a regiment or military unit.

To the poor persons of a particular religious group.

To such poor relations as the Executor thinks are deserving cases.

A gift to an institution, such as a religious order, is still charitable, if that particular institution works towards the relief of poverty of other persons.

Gifts for the Advancement of Education

These include gifts to particular educational institutions, colleges, universities, etc.; gifts for educating a particular group of people such as the mentally or physically handicapped; and scholarships, etc. Such gifts, however, must be for the benefit of the public or a section of the public in order for them to be regarded as charitable.

Gifts for the Advancement of Religion

This includes gifts for religious buildings, churches, graveyards, and burial places, religious books, organ and organist, missionaries, clergymen, etc. As in gifts for education, however, there must be a general public benefit arising out of the gift.

Gifts for Other Purposes Beneficial to the Community

This can include gifts which cannot be described under relief of poverty, advancement of education and advancement of religion. The important and essential element in these gifts, however, if they do not come within the other categories, is that they must be for the benefit of the general public and not for individuals.

The following is a list of gifts that have been regarded as being beneficial to the community, but the list is not exhaustive:—

gifts to promote certain ideas

 Conservative principles combined with mental and moral improvement;

 Socialism;

advancement of ideas of government;

gifts for encouraging national feeling;

gifts to promote the military and associated purposes (e.g. teaching shooting, the volunteer corps, officers' mess, regimental sport fund, defence from air attack, training boys to become Naval or Merchant Naval officers, prize for cadets, institutions for ex-members of the forces);

gifts for providing accurate law reports;

gifts for public works, building bridges, protection of the coast, repairing highways, public lighting, hospital, improvement of a city, convalescent home for children, public hall, public park, fire brigade, public library, public recreation, museum;

gifts for benefiting agriculture.

There are many others, but if you are in doubt you should consult a solicitor for his advice as to whether a particular purpose would be regarded as charitable or not.

Other Special Cases:

Foreigners

A Foreigner can receive a gift under the Will. If, however, there is a state of war and he is an enemy then he cannot receive a gift. Likewise, a person who was resident in an enemy country or territory occupied by the enemy would not be able to receive a gift under the Will. It is possible that these people could receive the gift once the war was over.

Minors

A minor is a person who is aged under 18. A minor is not allowed to own land. Consequently no land can be left in a Will to a person who is under the age of 18, at the date of the death of the person making the Will. If one wants to leave land to a minor who may not have reached 18 at the time of one's death then the usual method is to give the land to trustees on behalf of a minor.

A minor cannot be a trustee.

Mental Patients

There is no restriction on a gift under a Will being given to a mental patient or to anyone who is not in possession of all their faculties. It may be that someone has to look after the gift because the person receiving it is so unstable in the mind that he could not deal with it. The fact that someone is mentally unstable, however, is no bar to him being left a gift.

Trade Unions and Employers' Associations

Both trade unions and employers' associations are allowed to hold property which is held by trustees on their behalf.

Clubs, Societies and Institutions

A gift can be left in a Will to a club or society or other institution whether or not they are charitable. The gift can be expressed to be for the particular institution or, alternatively, it can be expressed to be for the members of the institution.

Companies, Corporations and Local Authorities

There is no restriction on a gift under a Will, including land, being given to a company or corporation or local authority. There may be tax considerations on a gift to a local authority.

Looking After The Grave

Some people will want to have a monument erected or maintained or to have their grave or memorial cared for after their death. Under an Act of Parliament a burial authority or local authority can agree to maintain:

(a) a grave, vault, tombstone, or other memorial in a burial ground or crematorium provided or maintained by the authority;

(b) a monument or other memorial to any person within the

area of the authority to which the authority have right of access.

If such an agreement is concluded then it cannot be for a period longer than 99 years. There is no duty on the local authority to enter into such an agreement and it is a matter for the local authority to decide whether it wishes to enter into such an agreement or not.

If a person wanted such an agreement whereby the local authority will maintain a grave or monument then he should have directed in his Will that his Executors should enter into such an agreement with the local authority. He should have ensured also that there is sufficient money for the local authority to be paid.

This applies to *any* grave, monument, memorial, etc., and not just to that of the person making the Will.

10
Scotland

Confirmation

Grant of Probate or Letters of Administration in Scotland is known as a Confirmation which gives the Executor or Administrator power to deal with the whole estate of the deceased situated within the United Kingdom.

If you have any problems then you should write to the Commissary Clerk, H.M. Commissary Office, 16 North Bank Street, Edinburgh EH1 2NJ. Telephone 031-226 7181.

The law in Scotland differs from that in the rest of the U.K. in certain important aspects. Moreover, there is a considerable difference in the procedure for obtaining Confirmation depending on the value of the estate. If the estate is £17,000 or over then you will have to do this through a solicitor in Scotland and the Commissary Office will inform you that they cannot assist. If it is under this amount there is a small estate procedure and you can obtain advice from a court or a solicitor empowered to administer oaths.

Firstly, it is helpful to look at what happens to the estate of somebody who has died without leaving a Will but having been domiciled in Scotland.

1. If there is a surviving spouse only and no children or other descendants, no parents, brothers, sisters or their children then the surviving spouse takes the whole estate.

2. If there is a surviving spouse and children the surviving spouse takes the house (or £65,000 if it is worth more than that) and personal belongings up to £12,000, any cash up to £21,000 and one third of the remaining moveable estate. The rest is divided equally among the children, or

any of their children if they have died. You should remember that any money given to a child by the person who has died during his lifetime will be taken off the amount he receives. (Note that Parliament could alter these figures and the up-to-date position should be checked.)

3. If there is no surviving spouse but children are alive then the estate is divided equally among the children which includes illegitimate and adopted but not step-children. If any have died then their share is divided up among their own children.

4. If there is no surviving spouse nor children but parents, brothers and sisters who are alive then half the estate is taken by the parents equally and half goes equally to all the brothers and sisters, or their children if any of them have died. If any one of these groups is available then the whole estate goes to that particular group. Half brothers and half sisters will only be entitled if there are no full brothers or full sisters.

5. If there is no surviving spouse and no close relatives then the estate is distributed to the following groups, in this order:

> full uncles and aunts or their children
> half uncles and aunts or their children
> grandparents
> full great uncles and aunts or their descendants
> half great uncles and aunts or their descendants
> great grandparents

If there are no relatives who can be found then the whole estate is taken by the Crown which may make gifts to people who may make a claim if they were closely involved with the deceased.

In Scotland obtaining Probate is known as obtaining Confirmation although there is no set procedure for it. Application is made to one of the Sheriff Courts. Where a person dies without leaving a Will application has to be made to one of these Courts for the appointment of an Executor who will be one or more of the persons entitled to share in the estate under the rules set out above. Persons so appointed will have to give security pending the discharge of their function as administrators. Such Executors or, in the case of a Will naming Executors, the named Executors, then have to prepare an inventory of the estate which is a list of all the items in it. The truth of this has to be sworn to in front of a Notary Public or a Justice of the Peace rather like an affidavit. It is on the basis of this information that the Inland Revenue assess the tax payable by the estate. The local Sheriff Court then has to confirm (hence the name obtaining Confirmation) that the Executors are entitled to administer the estate and this is done once the inventory has been deposited with the Court which, therefore, has a list before it of all the items in the estate.

Where the estate is small in value the application for confirmation can be made to the Sheriff Court Clerk who prepares the inventory rather than having to apply to the Court by writ. The Clerk will deal also with the other formalities. In the case of a small estate where there is no Will and a near relative is applying to be confirmed as Executor he/she will have to prove his/her relationship to the deceased which can be done by two witnesses giving evidence on oath to the Sheriff Court Clerk.

Obtaining a Death Certificate in Scotland

Within eight days notification must be given to the Registrar of either the District in which the death took place or the District in which the dead person was living. The Register must be signed in the presence of the Registrar by a relative, any person present at the death, the Executor or other legal representative, the occupier of the place in which the death occurred or any other person knowing the particulars. It is an offence not to register a death.

There must be a doctor's certificate of the cause of death and the Registrar provides a Certificate of Registration. This must be handed to the Undertaker prior to the disposal of the body if it is to be cremated but a body can be buried before the death is registered, in which case the Undertaker must give a Certificate of Burial to the Registrar within three days.

Inheritance Tax in Scotland

In Scotland there are strict legal rights that can be claimed by a widow or widower or children and these rights cannot be excluded by the terms of a Will.

On the death of a husband or wife if there are no children the widow or widower is entitled to claim half of all the estate's moveable assets, which really means all things such as personal effects, furniture and cars, but not land or houses or flats. If there are children then the widow or widower can claim one-third of the moveable assets which includes cash and securities for cash. Children have the right to claim one-half of the moveable assets of their mother or father who has just died if their other parent is already dead. They claim one-third of the moveable assets if the other parent is still alive. The widow or widower and children have to decide whether they wish to claim their legal rights, as set out above, or whether they wish to take property left to them in the Will according to the terms of the Will. They cannot have it both ways.

We can see from these rules that it is very difficult to disinherit a wife/husband and children because, after the death, they will be able to claim their legal rights. These claims, however, are against moveable assets only. Consequently, if a person were to sell most of his moveable goods and spend his money on buying land and houses then there would be very little against which a surviving spouse and children could claim.

If a person dies without making a Will. then, in addition to the legal rights set out above, a widow or widower has other rights which can take all of the moveable assets.

If a gift in a Will to the deceased's spouse encroaches upon the right of children to share in the moveable assets then the extent to which the estate is taken by the surviving spouse depends on whether or not the child(ren) renounces his legal right, which as a general rule he cannot finally do while he is still a minor. As far as Inheritance Tax is concerned the part of the estate affected by the child's legal rights is treated as not passing to the surviving spouse, so that tax is paid by the Executors on the basis that the spouse exemption is not available to that extent. If, however, the child subsequently renounces his claim, allowing the gift in the Will in favour of the spouse to take effect, tax is repaid to the estate on the basis that the amount concerned was covered by the spouse exemption. The tax repaid carries interest from the original date of payment at the rate appropriate to transfers on death.

Alternatively, the Executors may choose to pay tax on the death as though the gift in favour of the spouse took effect in full, and so obtain the benefit of the spouse exemption at the outset. If the child subsequently claims his legal rights, however, the spouse exemption is lost to that extent and additional tax becomes payable together with interest from the original due date at the rate appropriate to transfers on death. The child making the claim is responsible for payment of this additional tax and interest. Where the legal rights of more than one child are involved the additional tax is a rateable proportion of the amount which would be payable if the spouse exemption were withdrawn in respect of the whole amount of the estate which is liable to the legal rights.

A child can renounce his claim for legal rights but if he does not do this before or within two years of reaching the age of eighteen (that is ceasing to be a minor) then he is normally treated as having claimed his legal rights. Such a renunciation is not regarded as a transfer on which Inheritance Tax has to be paid. Where a child dies before the expiry of this period without having renounced then his Executors may renounce within two years of his death with the same consequences. Where this is done the legal rights will not form part of the child's estate for the purposes of tax on his death.

11

Inheritance Tax

Inheritance Tax was introduced on 18 March 1986 and replaced Capital Transfer Tax. It applies to deaths on or after that date and to certain gifts.

Scope of the Tax

A deceased person's estate consists of that person's assets held jointly as well as gifts from which the person still kept some benefit, and those assets held in trust in which the person had an interest. All these are liable to Inheritance Tax if they exceed the current threshold (in 1991/92 this was £140,000: see Appendix I).

How gifts are included

Added to these assets for the purpose of determining the total amount of the estate are any gifts (over and above the exemptions mentioned below) which were made within seven years of the deceased's death.

Rate of Tax

Inheritance Tax on any amount over the current threshold is charged at the current rate or rates (in 1991/92 this was a single rate of 40%).

Under the relevant Acts it is provided that the threshold must be increased from 6 April each year in line with the increase in the retail price index for the year to the previous December, rounded up to the next £1,000, although Parliament may further change this figure from time to time (see Appendix I). In the case of married couples, each spouse's gifts are regarded separately.

Business is excluded

Inheritance Tax applies only to gifts and not to commercial transactions. Thus, if goods are sold and a commercial price is paid for them there is no question of that transaction being brought into account for Inheritance Tax purposes. Even if the sale price is subsequently discovered to be too high or too low (for example where the true value of an antique is not fully appreciated) then no Inheritance Tax charge can arise so long as the transaction was not deliberately intended to confer such a benefit. You need not worry every time you go to the shops!

Lifetime gifts on which Capital Transfer Tax was paid

If any gifts were made before 18 March 1986 (but still within seven years of the deceased's death) then, if Capital Transfer Tax (the previous tax which Inheritance Tax replaced) was paid when they were made, the amount of Capital Transfer Tax so paid will be allowed against any liability for Inheritance Tax.

Any gifts made after that date between individuals are known as Potentially Exempt Transfers, and if the person making them dies after seven years from the date of the gift, will not be included in the estate for Inheritance Tax calculations. Even if the person does die within seven years of making the gift there is certain relief depending on the number of years left between the gift and the death. The amount is tapered in favour of gifts made more than three years before death. This is set out in Appendix I.

Gifts into or out of Trust

There are different rules for lifetime gifts made into or out of trust. If it is a gift to an approved "accumulation and maintenance" trust (such as for the education of children) or a trust for disabled persons then it is treated the same as a gift between individuals and is a Potentially Exempt Transfer.

If, however it is into or out of another kind of trust then it is taxed at the time it is made (currently at one half the full rate). If such a gift is made within seven years of death then, of course, it will become part of the estate and further tax will be payable (subject to the relief as to the number of years remaining between the gift and the death).

In these circumstances any tax paid at the time of the gift will be allowed against IHT charged on death. If, for example, a gift is made into a discretionary trust (which gives the trustees discretion as to how the trust funds are distributed) then a charge arises immediately.

Gifts with Reservation

Mention is made above of gifts in which the donor still retains some benefit. This is known as a gift with reservation.

House in which a parent still lives

The most obvious example is where the parent of a child wants to make a gift to that child of the house in which the parent lives. Under previous legislation this was treated as an absolute gift and the value of the house would not have been included in the parent's estate when that parent died. Under the present rules, however, so long as the parent resides in the house the parent is still retaining a benefit and, if the parent is still residing in the house at the date of the parent's death, the value of the house will be included in the parent's estate. It is a gift "with reservation". The test is that for the gift to be potentially exempt (a Potentially Exempt Transfer) the property must be enjoyed by the beneficiary to the entire or virtually entire, exclusion of the donor. The gift of the house in the example above would still be a Potentially Exempt Transfer if, say, the child lived in the house all the time with his family, and the parent came to stay from time to time on short visits.

Ways round the gift with reservation difficulty would be if the parent sold the house to the child for its market value, or purchased a lease of it after transferring it to the child, or paid a commercial rent for occupation to the child. But the financial implications of these options usually make them unattractive propositions. If, of course, the parent ceases to reside in the house before the parent's death (if, for example, the parent goes into a nursing home) then the gift becomes wholly exempt. But if that event takes place within seven years of the death then it becomes a Potentially Exempt Transfer and the rules about gifts within seven years of death apply.

This is the reason that on the Form Cap 44 (see Chapter 5 above) you are asked to list any gifts made within seven years of the death.

An example

All this is best explained by way of an example (always assuming that the current system continues with the current rates of tax and threshold as an illustration):

In January 1990 Mr Snooks makes a gift of £50,000
In April 1990 he makes another gift of £30,000
In March 1997 he dies leaving an estate valued at £160,000.

As the gift in January 1990 is more than seven years from his death it is not included in the value of this estate but the gift in April 1990 is within the seven years and is added to his estate making a total of £190,000. This means that there is an excess of £50,000 above the threshold of £140,000 and is subject to Inheritance Tax, though there will be benefit from the taper as shown in Appendix I (page 113).

Funeral Expenses

The cost of reasonable funeral expenses (which includes the provision of a gravestone or tombstone) is deducted from the value of the estate before Inheritance Tax is calculated.

Life Insurance Policies

If a policy is taken out by a person on his own life and for his benefit (i.e. the proceeds are payable to that person) then it will form part of that person's estate on death. If on his death the benefit passes to his spouse then it is exempt from Inheritance Tax under the spouse exemption. Also, if the policy is taken out for the benefit of another who survives the person taking it out then it does not form part of the estate. This is also the case if a policy for the benefit of the person taking it out is subsequently assigned to someone else.

If, however, the beneficiary dies before the person taking it out does then the policy will revert to that person's estate. The actual payment of the premium is a gift and is subject to the same exemptions and reliefs as other Potentially Exempt Transfers.

Business Property Relief

Relief at either 50% or 30% (see below) is available on certain types of business and business property of the deceased so long as it has been owned by the deceased for at least two years.

It includes the business of a profession or vocation. It does not include a business dealing in securities, stocks and shares, land or buildings other than in certain circumstances.

How the relief works

The way in which this relief works is to reduce the value of the business or property by the appropriate percentage in calculation of the deceased's assets for Inheritance Tax purposes. This, of course, can be most useful in reducing the amount of tax payable on assets over the limit of the current Inheritance Tax threshold. In some cases, it may even bring the valuation of the estate below the Inheritance Tax threshold, so that no tax is payable at all. The relief applies to assets given during the deceased's lifetime as well as on death.

Relief at 50%

50% *relief* is given on the valuation of:

1. the business of a sole proprietor or a partner
2. a life tenant's business or interest in a business
3. any holding of shares or securities which gives control (i.e. controlling the majority of voting powers) of a company (whether or not it is quoted on the International Stock Exchange)
4. unquoted shares which either on their own or with other shares/securities of the deceased give control of more than 25% of the votes of a company.

Relief at 30%

30% *relief* is given on the valuation of:

1. shares which do not come within the above categories and which are not quoted on any stock exchange
2. land, buildings, plant and machinery used wholly or mainly in the business and
3. such land, buildings, plant and machinery which was settled property in which the deceased had an interest.

Agricultural Property Relief

Relief at 50% is given to the value of agricultural land or pasture in the UK including farmhouses, outbuildings etc which are ancillary to it, stud farms for breeding and rearing horses and to grazing land associated with it. The relief is available even if the land is let.

It is not available, however, unless the property either was occupied by the deceased for agricultural purposes for at least two years or was owned by the deceased for at least seven years during which it was occupied for agricultural purposes. Where such property qualifies for both agricultural and business relief only agricultural relief is given, not both on the same property.

As far as valuation of the property is concerned it is the agricultural value and not any enhanced value due to the possibility of, say, planning permission being given for development on it. As in Business Property Relief the relief applies to assets given during the deceased's lifetime as well as on death.

Woodlands Relief

If the deceased owned woodland for at least five years before his/her death then within two years of the death an election can be made to exclude the value of the timber from the estate. If the timber is then later sold the value at the time of sale will be charged to tax instead of at the time of death.

Death on Active Service

If a member of the armed forces dies as a result of a wound or accident or disease contracted on active service then the estate is exempt from any Inheritance Tax normally payable. In such circumstances you should obtain from the Ministry of Defence a certificate to this effect. Similar provisions apply to members of the Royal Ulster Constabulary in Northern Ireland who die from terrorist activities.

Death at the Same Time

If two or more people have died at the same time (such as in an air crash or other disaster) then they are assumed all to have died at the same moment. In the absence of this provision the law has always presumed that the elder person dies first and, of course, this could lead to there being two charges for tax as the estate passes in quick succession.

One Death after Another

Even where people do not die simultaneously there may be a situation where an estate passes on one person's death to another person who then dies him/herself. If the estate is subject to the payment of Inheritance Tax on both occasions this could be most unfair.

Consequently, where the second death occurs within five years of the first then what is known as "quick succession relief" is available. Depending on the amount of time between the two deaths there is a scale by which the tax payable on the second death is reduced by a percentage of part of the tax payable on the first death.

Subsequent Fall in Value of the Estate

If the executors sell land, buildings or shares after the death of the deceased and they have fallen in value from the date of death then they are entitled to substitute the lower sale price for the original value.

For land and buildings this relief is available if the sale is within three years of the death. In the case of shares the sale must be within twelve months but must apply to the sale price of all the shares sold (not just the ones which have fallen in value).

How Much Inheritance Tax Will Be Payable?

This depends on five factors:

1. the value of the estate;
2. the value of Potentially Exempt Transfers (gifts made within 7 years of the death) and when they were made;
3. any exemptions from Inheritance Tax on the deceased's death such as that to his/her spouse, gifts to charities, political parties etc;
4. the current threshold above which Inheritance Tax is payable;

5. the current percentage rate or rates of Inheritance Tax.

It is important to ensure that you know the current rules and rates of the tax, exemptions, deductions and threshold as they change quite regularly.

Payment of Inheritance Tax

Inheritance Tax on a deceased person's estate has to be paid at the time of delivery of the account but, if not, is due within six months from the end of the month in which the death occurs.

If it is not paid by that time interest is charged from the beginning of the month following that in which the tax is due. There are arrangements for the payment of some tax by instalments.

Preparation of an Account

We have seen in Chapter 5 page 52 that, other than in the case of small estates, an account must be prepared. In general such an account must be submitted to the Capital Taxes Office within twelve months of the end of the month in which the death occurs.

If you are unable to provide the exact value of any property then you can submit a provisional account stating that the value on the particular item(s) is provisional. You must also give an undertaking to submit a further account as soon as the exact value is known.

Where you borrow money to pay tax due then the interest paid on the loan is allowable against the estate's income tax for the first year of the loan only.

How to raise the money

Once you have been notified of the amount of Inheritance

Tax payable you must work out how this will be paid. If it is small and there is sufficient cash in the estate it can be met out of this.

If, however, this is not the case you will have to make arrangements for raising the cash. You should approach the bank manager and ask him to open a bank account in the name of yourself and the other Executor(s). You should ask him for an overdraft to cover the amount of money payable in Inheritance Tax and Probate fees (as well as funeral expenses).

If the deceased had a bank account it is advisable to go to the same bank to open the account as, in many cases, the bank manager will allow an overdraft on the Executor's account to be covered by any money in the deceased's account.

Authority to Release Funds

Until Probate has been granted the bank manager has no authority to release any money from the deceased's account. Indeed, all the deceased's accounts (whether personal or business) will be frozen for the time being (money can still be paid in but no money can be paid out). Nevertheless, in cases of small amounts the bank manager may well transfer funds without first demanding to see Probate.

You should open this Executor's account at least two weeks before the interview at the Probate Registry so as to give time for the bank to issue a cheque book on which you can draw a cheque for the Inheritance Tax and Probate fees. The bank manager will be able to offer advice as to how best to go about such matters.

National Savings

If the deceased had Premium Bonds or National Savings Certificates or money in the National Savings Bank you should inform the Probate Registry staff as these amounts can be used directly to discharge the liability for Inheritance Tax and Probate fees.

The Interview

You should remember to take with you to the interview at the Probate Registry all the papers and your calculations and valuations relating to the estate so that you can deal with any questions asked. You should have some idea of how many certified sealed copies of Probate you will need (there is a small charge for each one).

Releasing the Assets

Once you have been issued with grant of Probate you will be able to have the assets of the estate released by showing it or sending it to the various places at which the assets are held. You will then be able to distribute the estate according to the Will or rules of intestacy.

Perhaps the first person to whom you will take the Probate is the bank manager so as to release any funds in the deceased's bank account. When sending the Probate, or a certified sealed copy of it, you should enclose with it a letter asking for the assets that are held to be released and to where they should be paid or sent. It is possible to do all this with just the one Probate document. Each time you send it to an institution holding the deceased's assets it will be returned to you with that institution's stamp on the back and you can then send it to the next one.

Advantage of having several Probate documents

If, however, you want to send out several letters at once you will need certified sealed copies so that one can be enclosed in each letter. Even in the most complicated estates with several assets and shareholdings you are unlikely to want more than half a dozen sealed copies.

Payment of Inheritance Tax by Instalments

In certain cases Inheritance Tax can be paid by instalments

and you should ask the Probate staff or Capital Taxes Office how much Inheritance Tax has to be paid before the grant of Probate or Letters of Administration can be issued and how much of the tax can be paid by instalments. Inheritance Tax payable on certain types of property can be paid by instalments. They are:

1. land and buildings wherever they may be;
2. shares or securities in a company if the deceased had sufficient of them to be able to control the company (which means that he had a majority of voting powers). In addition Inheritance Tax can be paid by instalments where it is in respect of shares or securities in an unquoted company and at least one fifth of the total amount of Inheritance Tax payable is in respect of assets which qualify for payment by instalments. Furthermore, this facility is available where Inheritance Tax is payable in respect of unquoted shares and the value exceeds a certain sum and they represent at least 10% of the company's share capital;
3. the value of a business or an interest in a business, which includes a profession or vocation, but does not include something which is done otherwise than for profit, such as a hobby;
4. timber.

If you wish to pay Inheritance Tax by instalments you must give written notice of the fact. The payments are of ten equal yearly amounts and the first instalment is due on the date when the whole tax would have been due if it were not being paid by instalments.

If you decide to pay by instalments and start to do so there is nothing to prevent you from paying the whole Inheritance Tax due in one lump sum at any subsequent stage. Generally, interest is payable on such instalments but not always.

Giving Property in Satisfaction of Inheritance Tax

Rather than paying Inheritance Tax in cash it is possible to give certain property instead. The Inland Revenue will accept land and buildings but this will be only where the land or buildings are of some particular interest, such as a historic house. If such a building is accepted in part satisfaction of Inheritance Tax then objects which have been kept inside it can be accepted as well if it is felt by the Treasury that they should continue to be associated with the building.

In addition, pictures, prints, books, manuscripts, works of art, scientific objects or other items can be accepted in satisfaction of Inheritance Tax if, in the view of the Treasury, they are of national, scientific, historic or artistic interest, and this could include a collection.

Saving on Professional Charges

You may find yourself the next-of-kin of someone who has died leaving a small estate but having appointed a firm of solicitors, or a bank, to act as executors and trustees.

There is usually a clause in the Will enabling such professional executors to make charges out of the estate for their services and this can involve several hundred pounds.

In such circumstances, if, having read this book and taken into account any complexities of the estate, you are confident that you could apply for Probate and administer the estate yourself, you should ask the solicitor or bank if they would be prepared to renounce Probate.

This means that they would not act as executors and would leave you to obtain Probate. This will save their professional charges and mean that more is available for the beneficiaries of the estate, the main one of whom may well be an elderly surviving spouse who needs every penny.

12
Deed of Variation

A Deed of Variation enables the terms of the Will to be altered so long as the beneficiaries get together and agree to the terms.

Obviously, a Deed of Variation is most likely to be of use where the existing provisions of the Will involve the payment of quite a lot of Inheritance Tax and the estate is a reasonably large one. A Deed of Variation can ensure that as little Tax as is necessary is paid. Consequently, if a Deed of Variation is likely then legal advice should be taken and the effect of the Will should be altered as soon as possible after the death of the deceased. A Deed of Variation can be effected even if it is not specified in the Will and this applies also to cases of intestacy.

A Deed of Variation, can be made by anyone who is a beneficiary, provided all the beneficiaries agree. It can alter the terms of the Will in so far that the estate can be split up in a different way other than described in the Will so as to gain maximum Tax advantage. Individuals can disclaim or release their benefit under the Will or intestacy.

This alteration or variation must be agreed by all concerned and drawn up in a proper document. The effect of it is that, for tax purposes, the altered and varied Will is treated as the original Will. Consequently, although there may have been heavy tax liability under the original Will in the way gifts were to be distributed, the Deed of Variation can change the way in which the gifts are distributed and so reduce or delay the tax liability. In the eyes of the taxman the Deed of Variation will be treated as though it is an alteration to the Will which was done by the person making the Will. This means that there will be only one transfer for tax purposes and not two.

If you think that a Deed of Variation would be beneficial, you should take legal advice.

13

What Happens if There is Not Enough in the Estate?

Hopefully, when you have taken into account all the specific legacies and bequests of money and property under the terms of the Will together with the payment of debts, funeral expenses and other outgoings there will still be some property in the deceased's estate which will be left over for which no specific provision has been made. This is known as the residue and most Wills contain a clause dealing with the residue giving it to a specific person or institution or charity. If there is property left over to form a residue and yet there is no provision in the Will as to where the residue should go then the residue will be dealt with according to the Law of Intestacy, that is as though the deceased person had left no Will in respect of the property comprising the residue. You should see Chapter 2 (page 28) so as to ascertain how this residue would then be divided up.

On the other hand, however, it may well be that the deceased person over-estimated the value of his estate and that there is insufficient property and money in the estate to pay the specific legacies and to make the specific bequests. As Executor, your first duty is to ensure that debts and funeral expenses are paid before payment of legacies. You would be quite entitled to pay legacies if you are satisfied that the amount of the estate is sufficient to be able to meet all debts and funeral expenses once the legacies have been paid. You have a year from the date of the death of the deceased person in which you can gather all the necessary information about the deceased person's estate and during that year you cannot be made to pay any legacies even though the Will might provide for certain legacies being paid within that time. You should remember that any application under the Inheritance (Provision for Family and Dependents) Act, 1975 by family or dependants of the deceased person for payment out of the estate must be made within six months of the grant of Probate or Letters of Administration. Once that six months has passed then there is no way in which a member of the deceased person's family or dependant can make an application under that Act without permission of the Court in special circumstances. Therefore, although you can pay legacies within one year of the date of the deceased person's death you are not obliged to.

Where the Will makes provision for specific items to be given to persons then you should try to keep those items and not sell them (in order to use the money from the sale or the objects themselves as payment for debts).

You should not pay a legacy to a minor. The payment of a legacy in favour of a minor should be made to the minor's guardian unless the Will specifically provides for payment to be made to another person, or where the minor ratifies the payment when he/she reaches the age of eighteen. Alternatively, the money can be paid into court or a Trust can be set up for the minor. Where a person who is entitled to receive a legacy is of unsound mind, then, likewise, that legacy should be paid into Court.

If all the legacies cannot be paid in full because there is insufficient in the estate then, unless the terms of the Will make specific provision as to how this difficulty may be overcome, then all the legacies should be reduced in equal proportions so as to provide sufficient for all the legacies to be paid in part.

If the deceased person in the Will has set aside a certain source of funds from which legacies should be paid then, if that source of funds is insufficient to pay all the legacies, you cannot take money or property from another part of the estate to satisfy payment of all the legacies.

Consequently, if the Will of the deceased person directed that Charles Bloggins and Samuel Bloggins should each be paid £5000 out of a specific Building Society Account and, on his death, there is only £8000 in that account then you, as Executor, must pay both Charles and Samuel Bloggins only £4000 each. Even though other money may be available in another part of the estate and there may be substantial money in the residue of the estate you cannot use this to pay both Charles and Samuel Bloggins the full amount since it was specifically directed that they should be paid out of that particular building society account.

The principle of reducing all the general legacies in order to make sure that they can all be paid in part, rather than some in full and others not at all, is known as abatement. This principle, however, does not affect specific bequests of particular property or money in the estate which is clearly identifiable. A specific bequest might include money rather than objects if it is clearly identifiable, such as money on a mortgage, money in a bag, or the proceeds of the sale of a specific house.

14

Examples of Wills

1. *A married man with or without children wishing to leave everything to his wife.*

This is the last Will and Testament of me Arthur Bruce Bloggins of 1 Whiteacre, Blacktown in the county of Greenshire, made this . . . day of . . ., one thousand nine hundred and . . .

I hereby revoke all former Wills made by me and declare, this to be my last Will.

I appoint my wife Ann Belinda Bloggins to be the sole executrix of this my Will.

I devise and bequeath all my real and personal estate whatsoever and wheresoever to my wife Ann Belinda Bloggins absolutely if she shall survive me by 30 days.

If she shall not survive me by 30 days then I devise and bequeath all my real and personal estate whatsoever and wheresoever to be divided equally among such of my children as shall be living at the date of my death.

As Witness my hand the day and year first above written.

**Signed by the said testator in
the presence of us, present at
the same time, who at his
request and in his presence have
subscribed our names as
witnesses.**

Arthur B. Bloggins

adam Smith

**of 2 The Cottages,
Blacktown
(Bricklayer)**

Milton Freeman

**of 3 Smallacre,
Blacktown
(Motor Mechanic)**

In this case the deceased person has appointed his wife Ann Bloggins to be his Executrix (that is the female equivalent of Executor) and has also left all his property to her. If you were the wife, Ann Bloggins, this would be a simple Will to administer since, once Probate had been obtained, you would be entitled to keep all the property of the deceased person which would then become yours absolutely for you to deal with as you wished.

You may wish to know why the absolute gift of all the property seems conditional on Mrs. Bloggins surviving her husband by thirty days. This is to prevent the situation where, say, both are involved in a car crash and the wife dies a few days after the husband. If there is no condition that she has to survive him by thirty days then, on his death, his property would pass to his wife but on her death, a few days later, the property would pass according to her Will or, if she had not made a Will, to *her* relations and not as the husband would have wished it.

2. *A married man with two children wishing to leave his wife a life interest in his property and, upon her death or remarriage, everything to his children.*

This is the last Will and Testament of me Arthur Bruce Bloggins of 1 Whiteacre, Blacktown in the County of Greenshire, made this . . . day of . . ., one thousand nine hundred and . . .

I hereby revoke all former Wills made by me and declare this to be my last Will.

I appoint Orlando James Clifford and Jonathan Glaze-brook Messrs. Smith, Jones and Browne of Peradventure Passage, Blacktown (hereinafter called my trustees, which expression shall include the trustees for the time being hereof) to be the executors and trustees of this my Will. My trustees shall be entitled to charge and be paid out of the residue of my estate all professional or other charges for all business or acts done by them in connection with this my Will.

I devise and bequeath all my real and personal estate whatsoever and wheresoever to my trustees upon trust to sell the same with power to postpone sale and to invest the proceeds thereof and to apply the income therefrom for the benefit of my wife Ann Belinda Bloggins until she dies or remarries, whichever is the sooner, and thereafter to divide the said proceeds amongst those of my children as shall be living at the date of my wife's death or remarriage, whichever is the sooner, in equal parts absolutely.

Notwithstanding anything herein expressed my trustees may in their absolute discretion at any time pay for the maintenance or benefit of my said wife any part or parts of the capital of the residue even though such parts may amount in the aggregate to the whole thereof.

As Witness my hand the day and year first above written.

Signed by the said testator in
the presence of us, present at
the same time, who at his
request and in his presence have
subscribed our names as
witnesses.

Arthur B. Bloggins

Adam Smith

of 2 The Cottages,
Blacktown
(Bricklayer)

Milton Freeman

of 3 Smallacre,
Blacktown
(Motor Mechanic)

In this case you will see that a life interest has been created for the benefit of the widow of the deceased person. This means that trustees have to be appointed in order to administer the life interest. Under the terms of this Will a local firm of solicitors, Messrs. Smith, Jones & Browne, have been appointed as both Trustees and Executors. They will be responsible for obtaining Probate and administering the Will. In addition to that, however, they have been appointed Trustees and they will be responsible for carrying out the terms of the Trust as set out in the Will. They are not expected to do this for nothing, and, as you can see, provision has been made for them to be paid for their professional services out of what remains of the estate.

They will be bound to carry out the Trust in the terms set out in the Will but you should see the chapter entitled "Trustees" in order to see what sort of things Trustees are entitled to do and what they should not do together with the powers that they have.

Although in this case solicitors have been appointed as Trustees there is no reason why lay persons should not be appointed as Trustees and you may well find yourself being both Executor and Trustee under the terms of the Will. You can refuse to be a Trustee although in a simple Will the duties will not be very onerous. Moreover, if you are to be appointed a Trustee under the Will it is most likely that the deceased person will have approached you during his/her lifetime and asked you if you consent to being a Trustee and Executor.

In the example of a Will set out above the Trustees have wide powers to sell the property in the estate or to keep it as it is and to invest proceeds of any sale of any property. They have a wide discretion in the way in which they can invest money although it is subject to the rules set out in Chapter 8 page 64.

During the lifetime of Mrs. Bloggins the income from the property and investments will be paid by the Trustees to her or will be used by them to purchase various items that she needs. In most cases the practice is that the income is paid over directly to the beneficiary.

You will notice also in the example Will set out above that a power is given to the Trustees to pay to Mrs. Bloggins not only the income from the estate but also amounts from the capital of the estate up to and including the whole of it if that is thought to be desirable in the absolute discretion of the Trustees. This wide power gives the Trustees the right to pay over or transfer any of the investments or property comprised in the estate to Mrs. Bloggins.

Although there is a provision in the Will for the division of what remains of the estate amongst the deceased person's children upon the death or remarriage of Mrs. Bloggins, nevertheless, if during her lifetime the Trustees have made over to her the whole of the estate in payments of capital then, obviously, there will be nothing left to pass on to the children. The Trustees could exercise their power in this way so that they could give everything effectively to Mrs. Bloggins and leave nothing for the children. If there is some property left, however, the Trustees will be responsible for dividing it amongst the children of the deceased person once Mrs. Bloggins dies or remarries. Once that division of property amongst the children has been made the Trustees' duties cease and the Trust comes to an end.

3. *A person wishing to leave a sum of money to charities to be selected by his/her Trustees. The relevant clause might read:*

> **I bequeath to my trustees the sum of £5000 upon trust to apply the same for such charitable objects or institutions as my trustees in their absolute discretion may select.**

Here there is complete discretion with the Trustees to apply the sum of £5000 for whatever charitable objects they wish. Consequently, the Trustees can give the money to one or more charities of their choice but they must be careful to make sure that that the money does actually go to a recognised charity and not to a body masquerading as a charity. If the Trustees were to give money to a body which was not properly a charity then they would be in breach of trust and could find themselves in serious trouble particularly if they acted in bad faith. The law relating to charities is far from simple and it is quite complicated sometimes to try to establish whether a certain institution or purpose is charitable or not. Consequently, if you find yourself as a Trustee with discretion to make gifts to charity then you should read Chapter 9 page 67.

4. *A Widow wishing to leave everything to her two children who are over the age of eighteen in equal shares.*

This is the last Will and Testament of me Ann Belinda Bloggins of 1, Whiteacre, Blacktown in the County of Greenshire made this . . . day of . . ., one thousand nine hundred and . . .

I hereby revoke all former Wills made by me and declare this to be my last Will.

I appoint my son Charles Alan Bloggins of 1, Whiteacre, Blacktown, aforesaid and my daughter Susan Rachel Bloggins of 2, White Cottages, Blacktown aforesaid to be the executors of this my Will.

I devise and bequeath all my real and personal estate whatsoever and wheresoever to my son Charles Alan Bloggins and my daughter Susan Rachel Bloggins in equal shares absolutely, provided that, if either pre-decease me, his or her children, if any, shall take that share in equal parts absolutely.

As Witness my hand the day and year first above written.

Signed by the said testatrix in
the presence of us, present at
the same time, who at her
request and in her presence have   *A B Bloggins*
subscribed our names as
witnesses.

Adam Smith

of 2 The Cottages,
Blacktown
(Bricklayer)

Milton Freeman

of 3 Smallacre,
Blacktown
(Motor Mechanic)

   This is a simple Will to administer since once all the funeral
expenses and Executorship expenses have been paid then all
the property must be divided up equally between Charles
Alan Bloggins and Susan Rachael Bloggins. As you can see
from the terms of the Will if either Charles or Susan dies
before the death of the person making the Will then his/her
child or children will take his/her share.

15
Definitions

It is important to realise that a Will is interpreted as describing property, people and other matters as at the date of the Will, and not as at the date of the death of the person making the Will.

Words must be given their ordinary dictionary meaning. Where the same words appear in different parts of the Will then it is presumed that they have the same meaning, although much will depend upon the context.

The following are some words which are commonly used in Wills, with an explanation of their meanings and pitfalls.

"beneficiary" — this means someone or something that benefits as a result of a gift in the Will.

"bequeath" — "I bequeath . . ." in a Will usually refers to personal property such as specific items, and money.

"children" — this includes both legitimate and illegitimate children and adopted children if there has been an adoption order. Where a gift is to a child and that child has children and dies before the death of a person making the Will then the gift will pass on to that child's children, provided they are living at the time of the death of the person making the Will and unless a contrary intention appears in the Will.

"Children" usually does not include step-children unless this is specifically stated, but "children" *will* include step-children where there are only step-children alive at the date of the making of the Will.

"Children" can also include grandchildren where it is clear that this was intended or there are only grandchildren and no other children are alive at the date of making the Will. But in order to save confusion the deceased should have always specified grandchildren where he/she wished to have them included.

"descendants" — this means children, grandchildren, great-grandchildren and so on down the line forever. A gift using this word is sometimes phrased as a gift "to my descendants living at my death" which includes all those who are alive at the time of the death of the person making the Will. "Male descendants" means males who are descended from females as well as those who are descended from males. A gift to "descendants" or "issue" means that all such take in equal shares. If the Testator wished each merely to take in default of a parent or parents then he should have added the words "*per stirpes*".

"devise" — "I devise . . ." in a Will usually refers to a gift of land (which includes a house).

"executor/executrix" — this is the person or persons appointed to administer a Will and to carry out the wishes expressed in a Will. Such appointment is done usually by a clause in the Will nominating the executor(s). Anyone can be appointed an executor apart from a minor or a person of unsound mind. A female executor is known as an executrix. A firm of solicitors or any individual solicitor can be appointed but they charge fees. Many banks have trustee departments and will act as executors and should provide a scale of fees. Many people appoint a relative who has some business expertise to be the executor since this saves on fees and moreover, because it is in the family, it may mean that the Will is administered more cheaply.

There is nothing preventing a person who is an executor also receiving a gift under the Will.

A person who is an executor cannot charge any fees unless this is authorised specifically in the Will. A bank or professional person is unlikely, therefore to accept the job unless the

Will makes provision for these.

An executor can decide whether he wants to do the job or not, and if he decides that he does not, then he can renounce it in writing. Nobody can force a person to be an executor. For this reason it is best to have two executors. If both decline to act then probate will be granted to the chief beneficiary under the Will.

"family" — this word is usually avoided as it has been defined in several different ways. It means probably no more than "children".

"husband" — this means the husband at the time of making the Will. In the event of a divorce a person remains married until the time of decree absolute (not decree nisi) and up until that time a person can properly be described as a "husband". Divorce does not invalidate a Will, save that any appointment of the former husband as an Executor or Trustee is treated as though it were omitted altogether. Moreover any devise or bequest to the former husband has no effect, unless the Will contains an express contrary intention.

In general, divorce does not invalidate a Will as a marriage does, but most people review the provisions of their Will if their marriage splits up.

"infant" — this means a child under the age of 18. An infant cannot hold a legal estate in land until he reaches 18, so land is usually given to trustees until he reaches that age. A pecuniary legacy is often given to a parent or guardian or trustees for the benefit of a person when he reaches 18 since he cannot give a proper receipt for it until he reaches that age.

"issue" — this means all descendants but has been interpreted as having several different meanings. In a simple Will its use is generally avoided.

"minor" — this has the same meaning as "infant".

"nephews" — much will depend upon the context of the Will as to what this means. It is best if the Testator has specified their names or their relationship with a particular person, such as "the children of my sister Katy". Remember, of course, that "children" includes illegitimate children and so, consequently, "nephews" could also include illegitimates.

"next of kin" — this means the closest blood relation.

"nieces" — the same applies as for "nephews".

"pecuniary legacy" — this is a gift of money in a Will.

"residue" — this means the amount that is left of the estate after effect has been given to all the gifts and testamentary and other expenses have been paid.

"survivor" — this may apply to persons who are not born at the time of the Will. For example, a gift to "my brothers and sisters who survive me" would include all brothers and sisters and not just those alive at the time of the Will. Similarly, a gift to "the children of my brother John Bloggins who shall survive me" even includes children born to John Bloggins after the death of the testator!

"testamentary expenses" — the deceased may provide for the residue of the estate to be left to a person or persons after the payment of all "testamentary expenses". This term includes the cost of administering the Will such as executors' expenses, investigations to discover the names and addresses of persons to whom payment has been left, any costs involved in taking legal advice or going to court in order to clarify the meaning of the Will.

A testator who wished to give his executors something over and above what they are able to claim as expenses in administering the Will should make a separate gift.

"trustee" — a trustee is a person to whom property is given in a Will to be looked after for the benefit of another person. This means that the trustee does not get the benefit of the property but merely holds it on behalf of the person for whom it is intended. If it is a sum of money, for example, the trustee may invest it properly and give the income to the person for whom it was intended in the Will. This is often done in the case of minors. If a sole trustee dies then the estate devolves on his personal representatives.

As you can see a trustee is someone who is "trusted" with another's property to look after it for that other's benefit. Trustees are usually persons who, the Testator felt, will deal properly and sensibly with the property. Anyone can be appointed a trustee apart from a minor.

"wife" — this means the wife at the time of making the Will. In the event of a divorce a person remains married until the time of decree absolute (not decree nisi) and up until that time a person can properly be described as a "wife". After the decree absolute, any appointment of the former wife as an Executrix or Trustee is treated as though it were omitted altogether. Moreover any devise or bequest to the former wife has no effect, unless there is an express contrary intention in the Will (this however, does not affect the right of the former wife to apply for financial provision under the Inheritance (Provision for Family and Dependants) Act 1975).

Appendix I
Inheritance Tax Rate

40% of the estate (including non-exempt gifts within seven years of death) over £140,000.

Relief on Gifts within seven years of Death (Potentially Exempt Transfers)
   The Tax payable on death on such gifts is reduced as follows:

Years between gift and death	Percentage of full rate of tax
0–3	100%
3–4	80%
4–5	60%
5–6	40%
6–7	20%

Exemptions
1. Gifts made between spouses, whether before death or on the death of the donor, are exempt. This total exemption does not apply where the spouse receiving the gift is domiciled outside the United Kingdom in which case the exemption is limited to £55,000.
2. Lifetime gifts not exceeding £250 in any tax year to any individual. Any number of gifts not over £250 can be made to different individuals.
3. In addition, lifetime gifts not exceeding £3,000 in any one tax year. This does not mean that you can give several gifts of £3,000 to different individuals, as the exemption of £3,000 is for a total of that amount.
4. Lifetime gifts which are made as part of the donor's

expenditure payable out of income. This should include subscriptions, medical insurance etc for another person but the result should not be to make a material difference to the donor's standard of living.

5. Certain lifetime gifts made on or before a marriage up to: £5,000 by a parent to a party to the marriage. For example, the father of the bride could give £5,000 to the bride and another £5,000 to the bridegroom. Likewise, the bride's mother could do the same. Moreover, the bridegroom's parents could make similar gifts. The net result could be that (so long as the parents are willing and they have the money!) both bride and groom could each go on their honeymoon £20,000 better off! Moreover, if the parents had not already made gifts of up to £3,000 (3. above) this amount could be added as well as a small gift of £250 (2. above) making possible the total gift of each parent £13,500. Fortunate indeed the happy couple who start their married life £54,000 richer and with no IHT to pay even if all their parents were to die the following day! One hopes, however, that the lives of parents are held more valuable by their children than even to contemplate such matters!

£2,500 by either party to the marriage to each other (although if both of them are domiciled in the United Kingdom any gift between spouses is exempt: see 1. above) or by a grandparent or other remoter ancestor of either party.

£1,000 by anyone else.

6. Lifetime gifts made for the maintenance of a spouse, children and dependent relatives. A gift for the maintenance of a spouse or former spouse is wholly exempt from any tax. For the gift to children to be wholly exempt then it must be to a child of either the donor or the donor's spouse and for the maintenance, education or training of

the child up to the age of eighteen or to the end of full-time education whichever is the later. The child does not have to be in the care of either parent for the exemption to apply and "child" includes illegitimate, adopted and step-children. A dependent relative is any relative of either the donor or the donor's spouse who cannot maintain himself/ herself due to old age or infirmity. Moreover, the donor's mother or mother-in-law is also included in the exemption whether or not she is infirm or elderly so long as she is not living with her husband. You should remember that the exemption applies only to the amount of the gift which is necessary to make reasonable provision for the relative's care or maintenance.

7. Gifts to charities in the United Kingdom. Do remember that not all organisations which may sound like charities are. You should ask if the charity has a registered number (although not even this is conclusive proof).

8. Gifts to political parties in the United Kingdom. In order to qualify as a political party for this exemption at least two of its members must have been elected to the House of Commons at the last general election or one member elected and at least 150,000 votes cast for its candidates.

9. Gifts to certain bodies which are concerned with the preservation of the national heritage or are of a public nature. These include national museums, universities and the National Trust.

10. Gifts of national heritage property to a non-profit-making body approved by the Inland Revenue. These include historic buildings, works of art and land of outstanding scenic, historic or scientific interest. There may be requirements as to public access and preservation of the property.

There are also exemptions and reliefs for business property, agricultural land, woodlands and gifts of land to registered housing associations.

Appendix II

Local District Probate Registries and Sub-Registries

(subject to alteration without notice)

The following are the district probate registries and sub-registries open from 9.30 a.m. to 4.00 p.m. Monday to Friday. Closed on Saturday. The local offices for each registry or sub-registry are in each case given below.

BANGOR 1st Floor, Bron Castell, High Street, LL57 1YS 0248 362410

BIRMINGHAM 3rd Floor, Cavendish House, Waterloo Street, B2 5PS 021 236 4560/6263 (COVENTRY, KIDDERMINSTER, LICHFIELD, NORTHAMPTON, WOLVERHAMPTON)

BODMIN Market Street, PL31 2JW 0208 72279 (TRURO, PENZANCE, PLYMOUTH)

BRIGHTON William Street, BN2 2LG 0273 684071 (CRAWLEY, HASTINGS, TUNBRIDGE WELLS, WORTHING)

BRISTOL The Crescent Centre, Temple Back BS1 6EP 0272 273915/24619 (BATH, TAUNTON, WESTON-SUPER-MARE)

CARLISLE 2 Victoria Place, CA1 1ER 0228 21751 (WORKINGTON)

CARMARTHEN 14 King Street, Dyfed, SA31 1BL 0267 236238 (ABERYSTWYTH, HAVERFORDWEST, SWANSEA)

CHESTER 5th Floor, Hamilton House, Hamilton Place, CH1 2DA 02443 45082 (RHYL, WREXHAM)

EXETER Eastgate House, High Street, EX4 3JZ 0392 74515 (BARNSTAPLE, NEWTON ABBOT, YEOVIL)

GLOUCESTER 3 Pitt Street, GL1 2BJ 0452 22585 (CHELTENHAM, HEREFORD, WORCESTER)

IPSWICH Level 3 Haven House, 17 Lower Brook Street, 1P4 1DN 0473 253724/259261 (CHELMSFORD, COLCHESTER)

LANCASTER Mitre House, Church Street, LA1 1HE 0524 36625 (BARROW-IN-FURNESS, BLACKPOOL, PRESTON)

LEEDS 3rd Floor Coronet House, Queen Street, LS1 2BA 0532 431505
(BRADFORD, HARROGATE, HUDDERSFIELD, WAKEFIELD)
LEICESTER Government Buildings, Newarke Street, LE1 5SE 0533 546117
(BEDFORD, KETTERING)
LINCOLN Mill House, Brayford Side North, LN1 1YW 0522 23648 (GRIMSBY)
LIVERPOOL 3rd Floor, India Buildings, Water Street L2 0QR
051 236 8264/8265 (SOUTHPORT, ST. HELENS, WALLASEY)
LLANDAFF Probate Registry of Wales, 49 Cardiff Road, Llandaff, Cardiff
CF5 2YW (BRIDGEND, NEWPORT, PONTYPRIDD)
LONDON Principal Registry, Family Division, 2nd Floor, Somerset House,
Strand, London WC2R 1LP 071 936 6983 (CROYDON, EDMONTON,
HARLOW, KINGSTON, LUTON, SOUTHEND-ON-SEA, WOOLWICH)
MAIDSTONE The Law Courts, Barker Road, ME18 8EW 0622 54966
(CANTERBURY, CHATHAM, FOLKESTONE)
MANCHESTER 9th Floor, Astley House, 23 Quay Street, M3 4AT
061 834 4319 (BOLTON, NELSON, OLDHAM, STOCKPORT, WARRINGTON,
WIGAN)
MIDDLESBROUGH 12/16 Woodlands Road, TS1 3BE 0642 244770
(DARLINGTON, DURHAM)
NEWCASTLE-UPON TYNE 2nd Floor, Plummer House, Croft Street,
NE1 6NP 091 261 8383 (MORPETH, SUNDERLAND)
NORWICH Combined Court Building, The Law Courts, Bishopsgate,
NR3 1UR 0602 414288 (LOWESTOFT)
NOTTINGHAM Upper Ground Floor, Lambert House, Talbot Street,
NG1 5NR 0602 414288 (DERBY, MANSFIELD)
OXFORD 10A New Road, OX1 1LY 0865 241163 (AYLESBURY, BANBURY, HIGH
WYCOMBE, READING, SLOUGH, SWINDON)
PETERBOROUGH 55 Westfield Road, PE3 6GS 0733 62802 (CAMBRIDGE,
KINGS LYNN)
SHEFFIELD The Court House, Castle Street, S3 8LW 0742 729920
(CHESTERFIELD, DONCASTER)
STOKE-ON-TRENT 2nd Floor, Town Hall, Albion Street, Hanley ST1 1QL
0782 213736 (CREWE, SHREWSBURY, STAFFORD)
WINCHESTER 4th Floor, Cromwell House, Andover Road, SO23 7EW
0962 53046/63771 (BASINGSTOKE, BOURNEMOUTH, DORCHESTER,
GUILDFORD, NEWPORT I.O.W., PORTSMOUTH, SALISBURY, SOUTHAMPTON)
YORK Duncombe Place, YO1 2EA 09046 24210 (HULL, SCARBOROUGH)

Appendix III

Probate Fees

There are two fees payable by the personal applicant: up to £10,000 you only pay a departmental fee; over £10,000 you pay the court fee *and* a departmental fee. The following scale combines the court and departmental fees payable on a grant of probate or Letters of Administration.

Unlike the different ways in which it is possible to pay Inheritance Tax (such as by the Treasury agreeing to take certain items in lieu of tax), probate fees must be paid in cash, either by cheques or notes, etc.

Where it appears to the Lord Chancellor that the payment of probate fees would involve undue hardship owing to the exceptional circumstances of the particular case, however, he is empowered to reduce or remit such fees.

Where any application for a grant of Probate is withdrawn before the issue of a grant, then the registrar may reduce or remit the probate fees.

Where the application for a grant is made by a personal applicant, such as yourself, rather than by, say, a solicitor, then the registrar may remit up to one half of the departmental fee.

Fees Payable by a Personal Applicant

Value of Net Estate	Fee
£ 0–500	£1
501–1,000	£2
1,001–5,000	£5
5,001–6,000	£6
6,001–7,000	£7
7,001–8,000	£8

Value of Net Estate	Fee
8,001–9,000	£9
9,001–10,000	£10
10,001–25,000	£40 plus £1 for every £1,000 or part of £1,000
25,001–40,000	£80 plus £1 for every £1,000 or part of £1,000
40,001–70,000	£150 plus £1 for every £1,000 or part of £1,000
70,001–100,000	£215 plus £1 for every £1,000 or part of £1,000

In estates of a net value in excess of £100,000 the following table of figures applies as a guide:

Net Estate	Fee
100,001–200,000	£300 plus £1 for every £1,000 or part of £1,000
Over 200,000	£300 for the first £200,000 and £50 for every additional £100,000 or part of £100,000 plus £1 for every £1,000 or part of £1,000

Extra sealed copies of probate, which can be very useful when administering the estate (if, for example, several companies in which the deceased held shares need to be notified at the same time), can be ordered with an additional payment of 25p per extra copy.

Appendix IV

Benefits for Surviving Spouses

Immediately after the death of a partner there is not only the emotional loss with which the survivor has to deal, and which can mean a mental inability to focus on practical and administrative matters, but also the problems for many of a shortage of money, either temporarily, until Probate is obtained and the estate is distributed, or permanently as there is the loss of the wage-earner; yet the bills still keep coming just the same as before. There can be very real diminution in the standard of living of the surviving spouse if there are limited funds in the estate.

There are various Social Security benefits which can help alleviate both these situations. They are all set out in detail in Leaflet FB2 "Which Benefit?" obtainable from Social Security offices, post offices, advice centres and by writing to the DSS Leaflets Unit, PO Box 21, Stanmore, Middlesex HA7 1AY. Listed below are other benefits besides Income Support, Family Credit and Housing Benefit.

Widows

A widow may get a *Widow's Payment* which is a tax-free lump sum paid immediately after death of the husband if he paid sufficient national insurance contributions and she was under 60 or the husband was not receiving a retirement pension at the date of his death. If you return the Certificate of Registration of Death, given to you by the Registrar when you register the death, the claim form will be sent to you.

A Widowed Mother's Allowance is available if you have at least one child for whom you are receiving child benefit or you are expecting a baby from your late husband or from artificial insemination. You may also be able to get extra help for those children for whom you receive child benefit and extra pension. Claim form (BW1) can be obtained from DSS offices. There are also various *maternity benefits*.

If you are aged 45 or over at the date of your husband's death with no dependent children or when Widowed Mother's Allowance ends you may be entitled to a *Widow's Pension*. At the age of 60 you would normally receive retirement pension. Claim on Form BW1.

If you are already receiving retirement pension this can be increased based on your own or your husband's sufficient national insurance contributions. If you are incapable of work you may qualify for *Invalidity Benefit*. If your husband died from an industrial disease or from an accident at work you may be able to get *Industrial Death Benefit* and claim *Industrial Injuries Disablement Benefit* for a period before your husband's death.

You should remember that generally you should make a claim within 12 months of your husband's death and that you will lose widow's benefits if you remarry or live with someone as your husband.

Widowers
The same considerations apply for retirement pension, Invalidity Benefit, Industrial Death Benefit and Industrial Disablement Benefit.

INDEX

RIGHT WAY
PUBLISHING POLICY

HOW WE SELECT TITLES

RIGHT WAY consider carefully every deserving manuscript. Where an author is an authority on his subject but an inexperienced writer, we provide first-class editorial help. The standards we set make sure that every **RIGHT WAY** book is practical, easy to understand, concise, informative and delightful to read. Our specialist artists are skilled at creating simple illustrations which augment the text wherever necessary.

CONSISTENT QUALITY

At every reprint our books are updated where appropriate, giving our authors the opportunity to include new information.

FAST DELIVERY

We sell **RIGHT WAY** books to the best bookshops throughout the world. It may be that your bookseller has run out of stock of a particular title. If so, he can order more from us at any time — we have a fine reputation for "same day" despatch, and we supply any order, however small (even a single copy), to any bookseller who has an account with us. We prefer you to buy from your bookseller, as this reminds him of the strong underlying public demand for **RIGHT WAY** books. Readers who live in remote places, or who are housebound, or whose local bookseller is unco-operative, can order direct from us by post.

FREE

If you would like an up-to-date list of all **RIGHT WAY** titles currently available, please send a stamped self-addressed envelope to

ELLIOT RIGHT WAY BOOKS, KINGSWOOD, SURREY, KT20 6TD, U.K.